Tokens & Traders of Kent in the Seventeenth, Eighteenth & Nineteenth Centuries

David Villanueva

Published by True Treasure Books
Whitstable, Kent, UK
ISBN 9780955032585

CONTENTS

1. INTRODUCTION

Coins traditionally contained the value of the metal from which they were made, less a nominal amount for the monarch and mint master and could only be produced by Royal decree. The original penny was made of silver and weighed $1/240^{th}$ of a Troy pound. That is why we had 240 pennies in our pre-decimal pound. Of course, as the price of silver rose, which it inevitably did through inflation, the size of the coin decreased until by the sixteenth century the penny and its fractions became inconveniently small, both to manufacture and use. Monarchs of the time had no desire to have their portraits engraved on a lower value metal so the general population had little recourse but to use token coins containing less than their intrinsic value of metal until the monarch provided sufficient usable coinage to sustain the needs of trade.

Trade tokens were issued, to alleviate shortage of small change, in three distinct periods, the first during the seventeenth century, 1648-1672 (1679 in Ireland). The second period of trade token issuing was in the eighteenth century (including the first two years of the nineteenth century), 1787-1801 and finally the nineteenth century, 1811-15. As well as being collectable, in their own right like coins, tokens issued by tradesmen, as opposed to corporations, contain personal information such as name, location, trade and even spouse's forename initial in many cases and will be of particular interest to genealogists as well as family and local historians. There is now a large group of regular finders of these tokens, metal detectorists, who will also be looking for a means of identifying their token finds.

A number of eminent numismatists (including Atkins, Boyne, Conder, Dalton, Davis, Dickinson, Hamer, Pye and Williamson) have studied these tokens and produced extensive catalogues, generally covering the whole of a series. Until now the only solution to identification was to somehow wade through one or more of these catalogues. The asking price for any of these catalogues, new (if available) or used can be upwards of £50 per volume. These catalogues can be borrowed free from the Public Library Service but there are few copies in circulation and waiting times can be very lengthy. It is true that as many of the catalogues were compiled in the 19th and early 20th centuries some have been scanned and are available online. The problem with scanning old texts is that the scanner has no real comprehension of what is written and so records what it perceives to be written and the result can be gobbledegook! A further problem, particularly with seventeenth century tokens is that genealogical information and full token details have been abandoned in more recent catalogues to keep the printing costs and cover price down. This serves the collector well but disadvantages not only the family and local historian but also the finder of excavated tokens where only parts of the detail may be visible.

The nature of tokens is that they tended to circulate very near to their place of issue so that the merchant concerned could exchange or redeem them for coin of the realm. While 18th and 19th century tokens did travel far and wide, especially those redeemable in several major cities, they remained common in their home county. Seventeenth century tokens generally only circulated within a seven mile radius of their place of issue. Seven miles was the typical distance between markets where the tokens would have been accepted. However, tokens issued near county boundaries would have also travelled into neighbouring counties, while London tokens travelled all over the Home Counties.

This book is written for casual finders, collectors, family and local historians interested in Kent. It catalogues all Kent token details available including all genealogical and local information recorded in earlier tomes (details of several taverns, inns, public houses and hotels have been updated). In all some 600 recorded seventeenth and around 50 eighteenth and nineteenth century Kent tokens are included, many of which are illustrated.

An illustrated section on popular token designs aids identification. Places of issue are listed alphabetically and within each place the surname of the issuer is also listed alphabetically. Using what you can see you will usually very quickly track the token down. You can quickly scan the text for any string of letters or numbers, design, quantities of lines, shape, unusual metal, value, etc. and providing it is a Kent token, I am confident you will find it!

4

2. SEVENTEENTH CENTURY TOKENS

The small coinage of Britain from the earliest times was of silver; transactions requiring money of low value were carried on by means of black money, turneys, Abbey-pieces, crockards, dotkins, staldings, and other base foreign currency, as well as by English leaden Tokens, all of which were illegal, and against the circulation of which many severe laws were enacted by our earlier monarchs. Silver money was coined as low in value as the penny, three-farthings, halfpenny, and farthing; all these were in common use, but from their small size and weight – the silver halfpenny of Elizabeth I weighing only four grains – they were extremely inconvenient and were easily lost. Small change of a more useful size and weight was required, even though it must consist of a baser metal. In the reign of Elizabeth, pattern-pieces were struck, and a proclamation drawn up, legalising the circulation of copper money; but owing to the difficulties the Queen had experienced in restoring the standard of silver money, which had been much debased during the extravagant reign of Henry VIII, her aversion to a base currency was so great, that the project was abandoned without trial. Pennies and halfpennies of small size, however, were issued in 1601 and 1602 for circulation in Ireland, and Elizabeth granted authority to the Mayor and Corporation of the City of Bristol, to issue a Corporation farthing Token.

The need for small change being urgent, Leaden Tokens, generally of poor workmanship, continued to be issued by tradesmen until 1613, the eleventh year of the reign of James I, who then delegated his prerogative of striking copper money to Baron John Harington, for a monetary consideration; the patent however was granted for farthings only.

On the accession of Charles I to the throne in 1625, the patent for the coinage of farthings was renewed. The privilege was grossly abused by the patentees, who issued them in unreasonable quantities, and of a merely nominal intrinsic value, the coins weighing only six grains each. They encouraged the circulation by giving twenty-one shillings in farthings for twenty shillings in silver; by this means many unprincipled persons were induced to purchase them, and would force five, ten and even twenty shillings' worth of them at a time on all with whom they had dealings. In a short time, not only the City of London, but the whole kingdom, and especially the counties adjacent to the metropolis – Kent, Essex, Suffolk, and Norfolk were so burdened with them, that in many places scarcely any silver or gold coin was left, the currency consisting entirely of farthing Tokens. The issue of this patent was one of the many arbitrary acts of the first two Stuart kings, which tended to destroy the attachment of the people to the Royal Family. It is remarkable that among the nearly 9500 Tokens described in Boyne's Work, the name of Charles is found on only 44. The numerous families named Smith, who issued above one hundred Tokens, have not a single Charles amongst them. James, being a Scripture name, has been more fortunate, though it is not so common as might have been expected.

The accumulation of the patent farthings in the hands of small tradesmen, caused the latter so great a loss, from the refusal of the patentees to exchange them, that in 1644, in consequence of the public clamour they were suppressed by the House of Commons, which ordered that they should be exchanged from money raised on the patentees' estates. Apparently an authorised currency was then intended, as two pattern farthings were struck, one of which is dated 1644; the design however was never carried out, men's minds being then too much occupied with, the Civil War between the King and Parliament.

The execution of the King in January 1649 put an end to the exclusive prerogative of coining copper and brass; tokens immediately began to be issued, and were circulated without authority, and, as stated on some of them, for "necessary change." As they were exchanged by the issuer when presented, they were far preferable to the patent farthings. The earliest date on the Tokens is 1648. Although those of that year are not numerous, they are found to have been issued in various parts of the country, and occur in sufficient number to lead to the belief that most of them were struck previously to the King's death; for though the year 1648 of the Old Style continued until March 24, 1649, (from the 12th century to 1752 the year began on Lady Day, 25 March) two months would seem too short a time for so many of them to have been designed, struck, and put in circulation.

During the whole period of the Commonwealth, no copper money was coined by the Government, except a few farthings, which are very rare, and were probably only patterns for an intended coinage. Silver money continued to be issued of the value of twopence, one penny, and halfpenny. That the government of the Commonwealth was as unpopular as that which it had overthrown, is evident from the Tokens, which were undoubtedly an index of public opinion: the Commonwealth Arms are very rarely found on them; whilst after the Restoration the Royal Arms, the King's Head, and other insignia of royalty, are exceedingly common.

The spelling of words in the inscriptions on the Tokens is variable owing partly to the lack of standardised English spelling at that period Dr Samuel Johnson's, **Dictionary of the English Language**, was not published until 1755) and partly to the ignorance of those who struck the coins. The word "halfpenny" offers a fair example:-HALF PENY, HALFE PENY, HALF PENCE, HALFE PENEY, HALFE PENNY, HALF PENIE, HALF PENNY and HAPENNY. The word "on" is often spelt ONE. We find also HIS DUBBLE TOKEN. The names of persons and of towns fare no better; HENNERE is put for Henry, ST. EEDS for St. Neot's, and SLAUGH-WHITT for Slaithwaite. One might have expected that on the London Tokens there would have been less departure from the ordinary spelling; but the metropolitan traders seem not to have possessed a greater amount of education than those of the provincial towns. On one London Token we find OLFA TREE for "olive-tree," on another "horse-shoe" takes the shape of HORES SHOW; Goswell Street appears as GOOSWEELL STREET, and Houndsditch as HUNDICH and HUENSDICH.

The coining of the Tokens seems to have been often performed by the Issuers themselves. In the 'Gentleman's Magazine,' vol. xxvii. page 499, there is an account of the discovery of a Token-press and dies, which were used by Edward Wood and his son Richard, of Chesterfield; they were found in their house after the death of Edward the son of the last-named Richard. The dies were cut on two small pieces of steel, each welded on a larger block of iron. The press consisted of four pieces of good oak, not less than four inches thick, very strongly dovetailed together. In the upper crosspiece was fixed an iron box and screw, on the bottom of which was one of the dies, whilst the other was received into a square hole made in the bottom cross-piece, where it lay as in a bed. The screw was turned by hand, in the manner of a capstan, by four handles, each about nine inches long.

For the convenience of recharging the numerous varieties of Tokens, tradesmen kept boxes with several divisions, into which those of the various tradesmen and corporations were sorted and when a sufficient number were collected, they were returned to the issuers, to be exchanged for silver. In the Metropolis the changing of farthings became a trade, and there are some examples of Tokens having been issued by Farthing changers.

There are numerous devices on the Tokens, which may be classed under the following twelve divisions:

I. The Arms of the Incorporated Trade Companies of the City of London. These were generally adopted by persons of the same trade throughout the country. The colours of Arms are not shown on Tokens and parts of the bearings are often omitted, with other inaccuracies. A description of these arms, frequently occurring on Tokens, will no doubt be useful:

Apothecaries; Apollo holding a bow and arrow supplanting a serpent. These Arms are sometimes not in a shield; occasionally the Company's Crest is used.

Armourers; on a chevron a gauntlet between two pairs of swords in saltire, on a chief an oval shield charged with a cross between two helmets.

Bakers; a balance between three wheatsheaves, on a chief wavy an arm issuing from clouds between two anchors, holding a balance. A frequent device of this trade is a wheatsheaf.

Barber-Surgeons; quarterly; first and fourth, a chevron between three fleams; second and third, a rose crowned. Between the four quarters a cross of St. George charged with a lion passant gardant.

Blacksmiths; a chevron between three hammers crowned. Frequently one hammer crowned is shown.

Brewers; on a chevron between three pairs of barley-garbs in saltire, three tuns. Two men carrying a beer-barrel is a frequent device of this trade. There are also many trade marks used.

Bricklayers; a chevron, in chief a fleur-de-lys between two brick-axes palewise, in base a bundle of laths.

Butchers; two axes in saltire between three bull's heads, two in fesse, one in base; on a chief a boar's head between two bunches of holly.

Carpenters; a chevron engrailed between three pairs of compasses extended.

Clothworkers; a chevron ermine, between two habicks in chief, and a teasel in base.

Cooks; a chevron engrailed between three columbines; sometimes only one columbine is used on the Tokens and not in a shield.

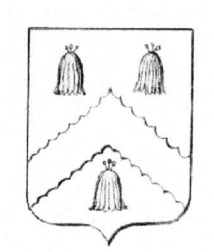

Coopers; on a chevron between three annulets, a grose between two adzes, on a chief three lilies.

Cordwainers; a chevron between three goats' heads erased; a single goat's head is also a device of this trade.

Cutlers; three pairs of swords in saltire, two pairs in chief, one in base, Generally on the Tokens the device for this trade is two swords in saltire.

Distillers; a fess wavy, in chief the Sun in splendour, in base a still. The Sun in splendour and the still, are each a device for Distillers, as well as dealers in strong waters; an Indian holding a bow and arrow, one of the supporters of the Distillers' Arms, is also used by this trade.

Drapers; three triple crowns resting on clouds radiated in base. One triple crown is frequently used.

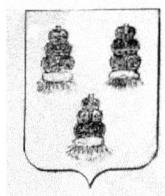

Dyers; a chevron engrailed between three madder-bags corded.

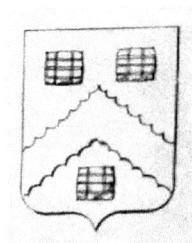

Farriers; three horse-shoes pierced. These are not engraved, as they are readily understood; the three horse-shoes are also a common alehouse sign.

Feltmakers; a dexter hand couped at the wrist, between two hatbands bowed, in chief a hat.

Fishmongers; three dolphins naiant in pale, between two pairs of pikes crowned in saltire, on a chief three pairs of keys in saltire.

Fletchers; a chevron between three arrows.

Founders; a vase between two taper candlesticks.

Fruiterers; on a mount in base the tree of Paradise environed with the serpent, between Adam and Eve.

Girdlers; per fesse and per pale, three gridirons, the handles in chief. The word "girdle" is still in use in the Northern Counties.

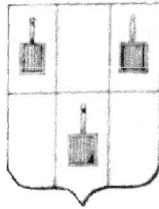

Glaziers; two grozing-irons in saltire, between four closing-nails; on a chief a lion passant gardant.

Goldsmiths; quarterly, first and fourth a leopard's face, second and third a covered cup, in chief two buckles.

Grocers; a chevron between nine cloves, three, three and three. These Arms are sometimes expressed by three cloves; one, two or three sugar-loaves are frequent devices of this trade. Admiral Smyth humorously describes a grocer of this period: "In country places a grocer comprehended a most extensive dealer in hardware, gingerbread, bobbins, laces, haberdashery, mouse-traps, curling-tongs, candles, soap, bacon, pickles, and every variety of grocery; besides which they sold small coins for money-changing. Tea, the staple by which grocers now make gross fortunes, had not then obtained its footing; for this lymph must then have been beyond the means of most sippers, seeing that in 1666 a pound of tea cost sixty shillings (£3.00) and money was then at a far higher value than now. The multifarious ramifications of those traders justified the application of the term grocers, as well as to those 'engrossing' merchandise, because they sold by the gross. Their more ancient name was Pepperers, from the drugs and spices which they sold; a branch which was mostly abstracted from them, not long before the epoch of the Tokens, by a seceding party, who were incorporated by James I under the designation of Apothecaries."

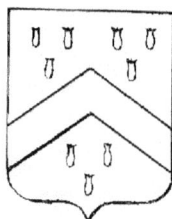

Haberdashers; barry nebulée, on a bend a lion passant gardant.

Innholders; a chevron per pale and per chevron, between three garbs. The Crest of this Company, a star of sixteen rays, is a frequent device of this trade, as well as a very common sign of an inn.

Ironmongers; on a chevron between three gads, as many swivels.

Joiners; a chevron between two pairs of compasses extended in chief, and a sphere in base; on a chief, a pale between two roses, on the pale an escallop.

Leathersellers; three bucks trippant regardant.

Mercers; a demi-virgin couped below the shoulders, issuing from clouds, crowned, hair dishevelled, all within an orle of clouds. The clouds are rarely seen on the Tokens, frequently the bust of the Virgin only is shown.

Merchant-Adventurers; barry wavy of six, on a chief quarterly, first and fourth a lion passant gardant, second and third, two roses.

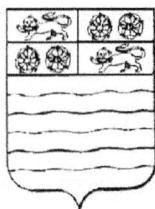

Merchant-Tailors; a tent between two robes, on a chief a lion passant gardant.

Needle-Makers; three needles in fess, each crowned.

Pewterers; on a chevron between three antique limbecks (alembics used by distillers), as many roses.

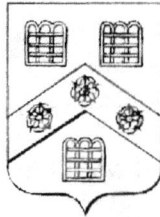

Pin-Makers; these Arms on the Tokens are the same as those of the Mercers.

Plasterers; on a chevron engrailed, between two plasterers' hammers and a trowel in chief, and a flat brush in base, a rose between two fleurs-de-lis.

Saddlers; a chevron between three saddles.

Salters; per chevron three covered cups sprinkling salt.

Shipwrights; Noah's Ark, on a chief St. George's cross charged in the centre with a lion passant gardant.

Skinners; ermine, on a chief three princes' crowns.

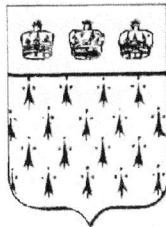

Soap-Makers; a dolphin naiant between three eel-spears;

Stationers; on a chevron, between three Bibles, an eagle rising inclosed, between two roses; in chief a dove displayed in a circle of glory. The device on Stationers' and Booksellers' Tokens is often a Bible, on others three Bibles.

Tallowchandlers; per fesse and per pale, three doves, each holding an olive-branch. The ordinary devices on Tallowchandlers' Tokens are, a man making candles, one or three doves holding an olive-branch, a stick of candles, and the same within a crescent moon.

Upholsterers; on a chevron between three pavilions, as many roses.

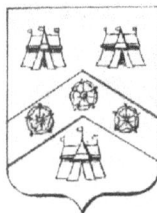

Vintners; a chevron between three tuns.

Watermen; barry wavy of six, on the middle bar a boat, on a chief two oars in saltire, between two cushions.

Weavers; on a chevron between three leopards' faces, as many roses, These Arms are frequently represented by three leopards' faces not in a shield.

Woodmongers; a sword erect enfiled with a ducal coronet, between two flaunches each charged with a faggot. On the Token of Govin Gouldegay, of Whitefriars, these Arms are a chevron between three faggots.

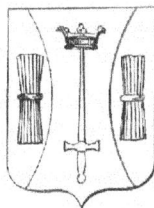

Woolmen; a woolpack.

In addition to the Tradesmen whose Arms have been described, the following have issued Tokens: Banksman, Baysmaker, Beer-brewer, Bell-man, Bodice-maker, Bookbinder, Bookseller, Broker, Capper or Cap-maker, Carrier, Chapman, Cheesemonger, Chirurgeon, Clerk, Clock-maker, Clothman, Coalman, Comfit-maker, Confectioner, Corn-chandler, Dresser, Farthing-changer, Flaxman, Flax-dresser, Gardener, Glassman, Gunner, Hatter, Hosier, Inn-keeper Limeman, Locksmith, Maltster, Mariner, Marshal, Mealman, Merchant, Miller, Milliner, Oatmeal-maker, Oilman, Patten-maker, Pipe-maker, Postmaster, Potter, Poulterer, Rope-maker, Rug-maker, Shoemaker, Shopkeeper, Silkman, Slay-maker, Smoker, Spectacle-maker, Starcher, Starch-maker, Sutler, Tanner, Tapster, Thread-maker, Throyster, Tobacconist, Tollman, Trunk-maker, Truss-maker, Turner, Victualler, Watchmaker, Webster, Wine-cooper, Woollen-draper, Woolcomber; as well as Bailiffs, Churchwardens. Lords of the Manor, Mayors, Members of Parliament, Overseers of the Poor, one Rector, and one Esquire.

II. Arms of Cities, Towns, Abbeys, the Nobility, and private families. These are fully described in connection with the Tokens on which they are found.

III. Merchants' marks. These are numerous. In early times, when few persons could read, these curious marks must have been very useful, to enable workpeople and others to distinguish the various bales of merchandise, by the particular mark, stamped on them. They appear to have been in use from the twelfth century; many of them are of a singular form, yet with all their strangeness they appear to have been used with considerable uniformity. Common devices of this kind are: a cross, the figure 4, a heart, a circle, and the initials of the issuer. The bale-mark of the East India Company was similar to No. 1, having in place of the letter S, the initials V.E.I.C. (United East India Company), divided by a saltire. Coats of arms, in early times not being allowed to men in trade, many merchant-families adopted their trade-marks in a shield, and these were continued by their descendants as an hereditary distinction; one such example is shown in No. 5. The Arms of the Borough of Southwark are only a trade-mark. In the seventeenth century these signs were falling into disuse and were not confined to wealthy merchants and ship owners, but were adopted also by shopkeepers.

MERCHANT MARKS AND UNCERTAIN DEVICES

IV. Taverns and Shop Signs. The earliest Tokens having been issued by publicans, they have, on that account, been frequently called Tavern Tokens. It is probable however that less than a fifth of these were issued by tavern-keepers. The usual device is the sign of the inn; the oldest of these signs were often of a religious character, as St. John the Baptist, the Holy Lamb, the Salutation of the Virgin (which had degenerated at that period into two men saluting each other), St. Alban, St. Hugh's Bones, the Cross Keys, etc. Some were of a loyal character, as the King's Head, the King's Arms, the Crown, the Three Crowns, the Duke of York (afterwards James II), the Royal Oak, etc. while those of a popular character were Guy of Warwick, Robin Hood and Little John, Friar Tuck, the Dog and Duck, the World's End, the Bird in Hand, the Hare and Hounds, the Have at it, the Jackanapes, the Hole in the Wall, the Cock and Bottle, Jack of Newbury, Will Somers, etc. The common alehouse signs of the Sun, Star, Still, Three Tuns, Wheatsheaf, and Indian (Belle Sauvage), are portions of the Arms of the Distillers, Innholders, and Vintners. Shops of all kinds were also usually distinguished by signs, which were highly necessary at a time when the streets were very narrow, and the houses were not numbered. Most of the devices in the next five categories were signs of shops.

V. Articles of Dress. sold by the tradesmen who issued the Tokens. These are interesting, as showing the fashions of the period. We find hats, caps, stockings, gloves, boots, shoes, coats, stays, neck-whisks, piccadillies, bands, leggings, pattens, etc.

VI. Implements of Trade, Agriculture, and War; such as axes, hammers, colliers' picks, woolcombs, hackles, croppers' shears, shuttles, teazlebrushes, tailors shears, scissors, currycombs, scales, measures, stills, windmills, millrinds, cogwheels, ploughs, harrows, spades, scythes, cannons, guns, pistols, swords, daggers, cuirasses, spurs, etc.

VII. Animals; as horses, oxen, sheep, antelopes, stags, goats, foxes, wild boars, bears, lions, cranes, swans, ostriches, peacocks, fishes, lobsters, etc.

VIII. Articles of Domestic Use; as fleshpots, blackjacks, tankards, coffeepots, tobacco-pipes, frying-pans, gridirons, knives, cleavers, tennis bat and ball, etc.

IX. Heraldic Signs; as a pheon, fleur-de-lis, unicorn, flying horse, phoenix, griffin, the fleece, portcullis, crosses of various kinds,Catherine-wheel, eagle and child, the three legs of Man, a sheaf of arrows, etc.

X. Conveyances; as coaches, carts, wagons and packhorses, ships, fishing and passenger boats.

XI. Views of Public Edifices; as churches, castles, bridges, etc. These are mostly unlike the structures represented.

XII. Punning Devices on the issuers' names, after the manner of canting heraldry; as examples, we have the following names each represented by the object: Archer, Bell, Bird, Buck, Buckle, Bull, Bush (a thornbush), Colte (a horse), Cox (two cocks), Crane, Curtis (two men curtseying), Fox, Hancock (a hand and a cock), Harbottle (a bottle on a hare), Hive (a bee-hive), Lamb, Partridge, Raven, Rook, Samson (Samson standing), Towers (a tower), Yate (a gate), Woodcock, Wren, etc.

The earliest dates are 1648, 1649, and 1650; but Tokens of these years are scarce; after 1650, until 1660, they are more plentiful, and nearly the whole of them are farthings; halfpennies are few in number; and there are no pennies. Those of a date subsequent to the Restoration of Charles II are the most abundant; halfpennies are very common and there are a good number of pennies. The years 1665, 1666, 1667, 1668, and 1669 are the most prolific, in particular 1666 (the year of the great Fire of London); whilst in 1670, 1671, and 1672 they again become scarce; of the latter year there are very few.

The Tokens were in circulation a quarter of a century; they originated with a public necessity, but in the end became a nuisance; they were issued by nearly every tradesman as a kind of advertisement, and being only payable at the shop of the issuer, they were very inconvenient. The Government had for some time intended the circulation of royal copper money, as there are pattern pieces of halfpennies and farthings of the year 1665; but it was not until the year 1672 that the farthings of Charles II were ready for circulation. Tradesmen's Tokens were then proclaimed illegal. This put a stop to the circulation of Tradesmen's Tokens almost immediately; a few attempts were made to continue them, but the threat of Government proceedings against the offenders effectually put them down and they disappeared into history.

3. EIGHTEENTH AND NINETEENTH CENTURY TOKENS

After the seventeenth century token issue, the government reluctantly took on the responsibility of producing regal copper coins but the obsolete machinery at the Royal Mint became increasingly unable to supply the demands of an expanding industrial society. From 1742 industrialists in Birmingham began producing an imitation copper coinage which was lightweight and deliberately miss-copied the regal coinage to avoid counterfeiting penalties. These were called 'evasions' or 'Brummagens' and towards the end of the eighteenth century they represented about three-quarters of copper coins in circulation.

Thomas Williams, owner of the Parys Mines in Anglesey, commenced producing good quality tokens in 1787, to alleviate the problem, with other industrialists following suit and this continued to around 1801, when a government re-coinage of 1797 had taken effect. So again you get a variety of traders, usually the wealthier, issuing tokens with their names and other details on.

But it doesn't stop there, the new coinage contained the full value of copper, the price of copper doubled by 1805 and it became very profitable to melt the coins down. There was a re-coinage in 1805 & 1807 but the distribution system was lopsided causing gluts and shortages resulting in another crop of copper tokens between 1810 and 1817.

There was also a shortage of silver coins as the mint hadn't issued any silver coins since 1787. The first expediency was to counter-mark Spanish silver dollars captured from Spanish Frigates. The Bank of England officially counter-marked large numbers of them and the traders did their bit too.

The countermarked dollars failed to keep up with the demand, so the Bank of England issued dollars and lightweight silver bank tokens in 3 shillings and 18 pence values and traders followed suit with silver tokens in various values. There was a major re-coinage in 1816, which, together with acts of parliament, brought a final end to all unofficial token coinage.

4. KENT

The map of 1868 shows Kent, as it was during the token issuing periods. Bexley, Bromley, Deptford, Eltham, Greenwich, Orpington and Woolwich, which were in Kent and have tokens listed here, have all been absorbed into London by the boundary reorganisations of 1899, 1965 and 1974.

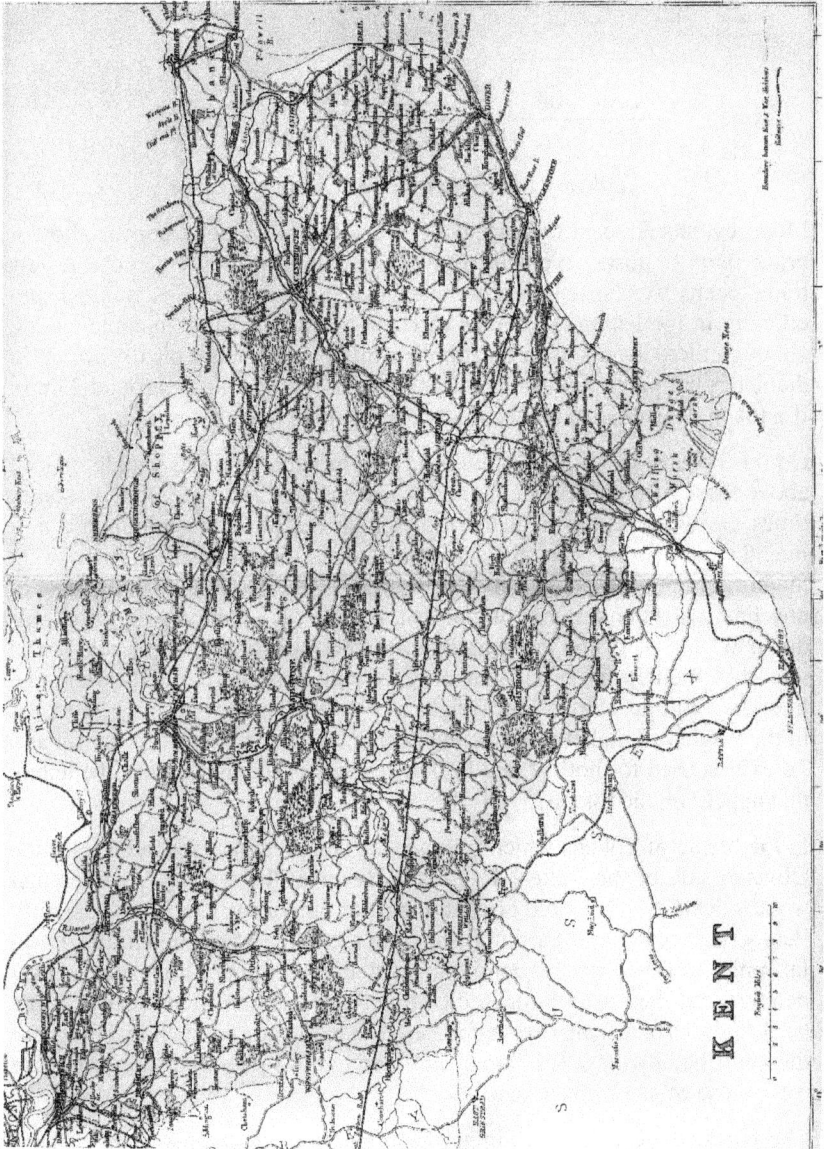

5. SEVENTEENTH CENTURY TOKENS OF KENT

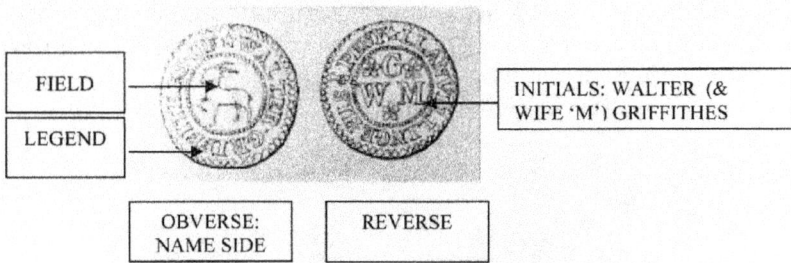

| FIELD | | INITIALS: WALTER (& WIFE 'M') GRIFFITHES |
| LEGEND | | |

| OBVERSE: NAME SIDE | REVERSE |

Anatomy of a Seventeenth Century Token

Most seventeenth century tokens are struck on thin copper, copper-alloy or brass flans or discs, typically only around one millimetre thick. A few trade tokens were struck in other metals such as lead and this is noted specifically in the listing. Diameter varies according to value to some extent, although there is no standardisation. Farthing tokens are typically 15mm in diameter; halfpenny tokens: about 20mm and penny tokens: around 23mm. If a token doesn't state a value then it is assumed to be a farthing.

On the Tokens, when initials are used, the surname initial is usually placed above those of the Christian names of the husband and wife; though sometimes the wife's initial is at the top, sometimes the three initials are in a line, the middle one being the surname, and at other times the surname is at the bottom. For the convenience of printing, the three initials are placed in one line, with the surname initial last. So the token above would be rendered W. M. G. If you are searching this book for initials on a token it is vital that you use that order. The only exception is where initials are in one line, they will be written left to right as viewed. There were only 24 letters in the English alphabet until the eighteenth century, I is used for both I and J and V is used for both V and U. The legends in the listings use the letters that appear on the tokens.

In the listing of Tokens which follows, the contractions used, are **O.** for the Obverse side of the Token, **R.** for the Reverse; the = mark signifies that what follows is in the field or central part of the token; 1, ½, and ¼, signify Penny, Halfpenny and Farthing, showing the value of the token; the Town farthings however are frequently larger than the ordinary tradesmen's halfpennies, but they usually have the value expressed on them: a few of the tradesmen's Tokens also are much larger than the others; such instances are distinguished by the word "large" prefixed to the value, to distinguish them from those of an ordinary size.

There is a convention of retaining the numbering from: George C Williamson, **Tokens Issued in the Seventeenth Century in England, Wales, and**

Ireland by Corporations, Merchants, Tradesmen, Etc. A New and Revised Edition of William Boyne's Work, and I have adhered to that convention here. As a result of new information some numbers are vacant, where the token has been reallocated to a different place or county. New finds are given the Williamson number of the preceding token followed by the suffix. **.1, .2**, etc. Michael Dickinson uses the suffixes a, b, etc. in his recent **Seventeenth Century Tokens of the British Isles and Their Values**, but it should be easy enough to convert **.1** to **a** etc. if you want to cross reference with that volume. Unfortunately there is a lack of full information on many of the new additions, so the listing may not be totally correct. If you come across a token that doesn't match the listing I would be grateful if you would let me know so that I can make any necessary corrections or additions.

The organisation of the token listings that follow are alphabetical order of place name using the 26 letter alphabet with modern spelling. Within each place tokens are listed alphabetically by surname of the issuer after any town Tokens.

Images labelled PAS are reused, with thanks, from the Portable Antiquities Scheme (PAS) http://www.finds.org.uk under a Creative Commons CC BY attribution licence. The full record can be accessed from the PAS database using the record identification code included with the image.

APPLEDORE

1. **O.** IOHN. BOVRNE. 1669 = Arms of France and England quarterly, crowned. **R.** OF. APPLEDORE = I. S. B. HIS DOVBLE TOKEN. (½)

ASHFORD

2. **O.** IAMES. BASSETT = St. George and the dragon. **R.** IN. ASHFORD. 1669 = HIS HALF PENY. (½)

The George Inn is still in Ashford.

3. **O.** FRANCES. BAYLEF. AT. THE = A bull. **R.** PYD. BVLL. IN. ASHFORD = F. I. B. (¼)

4. **O.** WILLIAM. BOTTING. 1669 = A malt-shovel. **R.** OF. ASHFORD. IN. KENT = HIS HALF PENY. W. S. B. (½)

5. **O.** BENIAMIN. BOWYER = The Haberdashers' Arms. **R.** IN. ASH-FORD. 1664 = HIS HALF PENY. (½)

6. **O.** JAMES. CHITTENDEN = A drinking-pot. I. M. C. **R.** OF. ASH-FORD. 1669 = HIS HALF PENY. (½)

7. **O.** THOMAS. CLERKE. AT. YE. PYD = A bull. **R.** BVLL, IN. ASH-FORD. 1668 = HIS HALF PENY. T. E. C. (½)

8. **O.** IOHN. DENN. 1669 = HIS HALF PENY. **R.** OF. ASHFORD = I. M. D. (½)

9. **O.** THOMAS. FENNER. AT = The Grocers' Arms. **R.** ASHFORD. IN. KENT. 57. = T. M. F. (¼)

10. **O.** THOMAS. FLINT = 1664. **R.** IN. ASHFORD = T. S. F. (¼)

11. **O.** WILLIAM. OSBORNE = The Grocers' Arms. R. **OF.** ASHFORD. 1663 = W. P. O. (¼)

Richard Osborne, of Ashford, was the father of Sir Edward Osborne, Lord Mayor of London in 1560.

12. **O.** THOMAS. REDFEILD = Checkers. **R.** OF. ASHFORD. IN. KENT. = T. A. R. (¼)

13. A variety reads RUDFEILD.

The Chequers Inn was pulled down many years ago; it stood on the north-east side of the church.

14. **O.** MARY. STEED = HER HALF PENY. **R.** IN. ASHFORDE = M. S. 1669. (½)

15. **O.** ROBERT. WAGE. 1668 = R. M. W. **R.** OF. ASHFORD. IN. KENT = HIS HALF PENY. (½)

16. **O.** ROBERT. WALBE. OF = A pair of shears **R.** ASHFORD. IN. KENT. 69 = HIS HALFE PENY. (*Octagonal*). (½)

17. **O.** HEN. WISE. HIS. HALF. PENY = The Grocers' Arms. **R.** IN. ASHFORD. 1664 = H. E. W. (½)

18. **O.** SAMVELL. WOOD. 1666 = A Saracen's head. **R.** AT. ASHFORD. IN. KENT = HIS HALF PENY. (½)

Sainsbury's supermarket now stands on the site of The Saracen's Head at the junction of North Street and High Street.

AYLESFORD

20. **O.** EDMON. SMITH. IN = The Grocers' Arms. **R.** ALSFORD. IN. KENT = E. M. S. (¼)

BENENDEN

21. **O.** RICHARD. GRANT. OF = The Grocers' Arms. **R.** BENENDEN. IN. KENT = R. M. G. (¼)

BEXLEY

22. **O.** IOHN. THORNDELL. IN. BECKSLEY = An ox and axe. **R.** IN. KENT. HIS. HALFE. PENY = I. S. T. 1667. (½)

BIDDENDEN

23. **O.** RICHARD. FOSTER. 1668 = A lion rampant. **R.** IN. BID-DENDEN. IN. KENT = HIS HALF PENNY. (½)

24. **O.** RICH. FOSTER. OF. BIDDENDEN = A lion rampant. **R.** IN. KENT. HIS. HALFE. PENY = R. I. F. The first two letters conjoined. (½)

25. **O.** ALEXANDER. HOMESBY = HIS HALFE PENNY. **R.** IN. BID-DENDEN. IN. KENT = A. H. H. (½)

26. **O.** ALIXANDER. HOLMSBY = 1658. **R.** OF. BEDDENDEN. IN. KENT = A. H. (¼)

27. **O.** ALEXANDER. LINDRIDGE = HIS HALF PENY. **R.** OF. BID-DENDEN. 1671 = A. M. L. (½)

28. **O.** THOMAS. SCEELLES = A ship. **R.** IN. BIDDENDEN. 1666 = T. M. S. (¼)

BRASTED

29. **O.** WILLIAM. LINES = 1666. **R.** BRESTED. IN. KENT = W. M. L. (¼)

BRENCHLEY

30. **O.** WILLIAM. WOODGAT = The Grocers' Arms. **R.** OF. BRENCHLY. 1654 = W. M. W. (¼)

31. **O.** WILLIAM. WOODGAT = 1659. **R.** OF. BRENCHLY. 1654 = W. M. W. (¼)

This is a singular token, having two dates. William Woodgate must have got short of his 1654 farthings and in 1659 used the old reverse die for his new tokens.

32. **O.** WILLIAM. WOODGATE. 1664 (in three lines; date below name). **R.** IN. BRENCHLEY = W. M. W. (½)

32.1. **O.** WILLIAM. WOODGATE. 1664 (in three lines; date between name). **R.** IN. BRENCHLEY = W. M. W. (½)

33. **O.** WILLIAM. WOODGATE. 1667 (in three lines). **R.** IN. BRENCHLEY = HIS HALFE PENNY. (½)

BROMLEY

34. **O.** THOMAS. GHOST. AT. THE = A hart lodged. **R.** IN. BROMLY. IN. KENT = HIS HALF PENY. (½)

35. **O.** ROBERT. KINGE. IN = Two keys crossed. **R.** BROMLEY. IN. KENT = R. M. K. (¼)

36. **O.** MICAELL. LEE. AT. WHITE = A hart lodged. **R.** IN. BRVMLEY. 1664 = M. E. L. (¼)

The White Hart stood just south of the Market Square until it was pulled down in the 1960s. It was a large inn well used in the old coaching days. Michael Lee was sent to Fleet Prison for debts to his vintner.

37. **O.** IOHN. PERCIVALL. OF. 1667 = A roll of tobacco. **R.** BRVMLEY. HIS. HALF. PENY = I. E. P. (½)

38. **O.** WILLIAM. WALDRON. OF. BRVMLY = A man making candles. **R.** IN. KENT. HIS. HALF. PENNY = W. A. W. (½)

BROOKLAND

39. **O.** IOHN. EVE. AT. 1671 = The Grocers' Arms.

R. BROOKLINE. GROCER = I. K. E. ½. (½)

40. **O.** IOHN. EVE = The Grocers' Arms. **R.** IN. BROOKLAND = I. K. E. (¼)

41. **O.** IOHN. HARRISON. BRUCKLAND (in four lines). **R.** A goat = I. H. (½)

CANTERBURY

42. **O.** THO. BAKER. CHEESMONGR = A hand holding a pair of scales. **R.** OF. CANTERBVRY. 1667 = HIS DVBBLE TOAKEN. (½)

43. **O.** FRANCIS. BANICK = A wheatsheaf. **R.** IN. CANTERBVRY = F. M. B. (¼)

44. **O.** THOMAS. BEST. COOPER = The Vintners' Arms. **R.** IN. CANTERBVRYE. 1650 = T. M. B. (¼)

45. **O.** THO. BVLLOCK. AT. THE. BVLL = A bull's head. **R.** HEAD. IN. CANTERBVRY = T. B. (¼)

46. **O.** THOMAS. BVRDEN. OF = A Vase of flowers. **R.** CANTERBVRY. 1667 = HIS HALFE PENNY. T. V. B. (½)

47. **O.** IOHN. CARDON. IN = A roll of bread. **R.** CANTERBVRY. 1656 = I. D. C. (¼)

48. **O.** HENRY. CARPENTER = 1667. **R.** IN. CANTERBVRY = HIS HALF PENY. (½)

49. **O.** HENREY. CARPENTER = 1658. **R.** IN. CANTERBERY = H. S. C. (¼)

50. **O.** IAMES. CHEEVER = A hand holding a pair of shears. **R.** IN. CANTERBVRY. 1663 = HIS HALF PENY. (½)

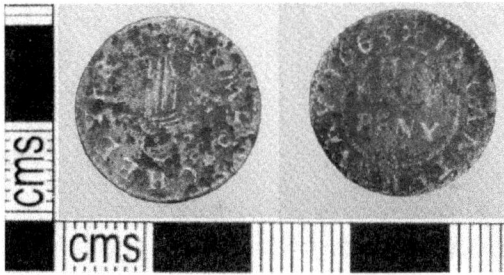

51. **O.** IAMES. CHEEVER = A hand holding a pair of shears. **R.** IN. CANTERBVRY 57 = I. C. (¼)

52. Another is dated 62. (¼)

53. **O.** EDWARD. CRAYFORD. IN = A black boy smoking. **R.** CANTERBVRY. GROCER = E. B. C. (¼)

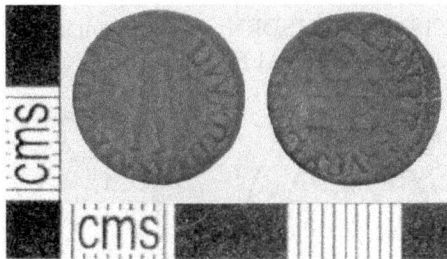

54. **O.** THO. ENFIELD. IN. MERCERY = The Grocers' Arms. **R.** LANE. IN. CANTERBVRY. 1666 = HIS HALF PENY. (½)

55. **O.** THOMAS. ENFIELD. IN. MERCERY = The Grocers' Arms. **R.** LANE. IN. CANTERBVRY. 1666 = T. S. E. (¼)

Thomas Enfield was mayor of Canterbury in 1674.

56. **O.** ANTHONY. FAGG. GROCER = The Grocers' Arms. **R.** IN. CANTERBVRY = A. M. F. (¼)

57. **O.** THOMAS. FEILD. IN = A Saracen's head. **R.** CANTERBVRY. 1666 = HIS HALF PENY. (½)

58. **O.** EDWARD. FRAY. IN = The Tallowchandlers' Arms. **R.** CANTERBVRY. 1667 = HIS HALF PENY. E. S. F. (½)

59. **O.** THOMAS. HVTTEN. PEVTERER = The Pewterers' Arms. **R.** IN. CANTERBERY. 1669 = A griffin. 1d. (*Octagonal*) (1)

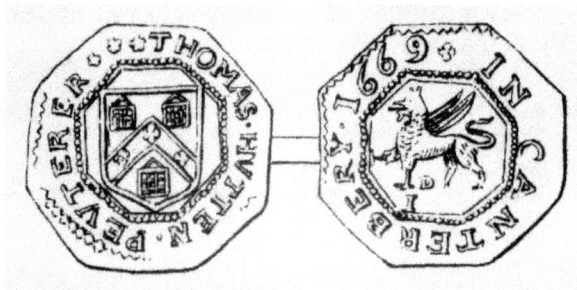

60. **O.** THOMAS. IENINGES = HIS HALF PENY. **R.** OF. CANTERBVRY. 1669 = A man smoking and making candles. (½)

61. **O.** THOMAS. IENINGS. OF = The Grocers' Arms. **R.** CANTERBVRY. GROCER = T. B. I. (¼)

61.1. **O.** THOMAS. IENINGE. = The Grocers' Arms. (*In lead*) (¼)

62. **O.** AT. THE. SHIP. IN = A ship. **R.** CANTERBERY. 1653 = M. S. K. (¼)

63. **O.** FRANCIS. MAPLISDEN = A bunch of hops. **R.** IN. CANTERBVRY. 1666 = HIS HALF PENY. (½)

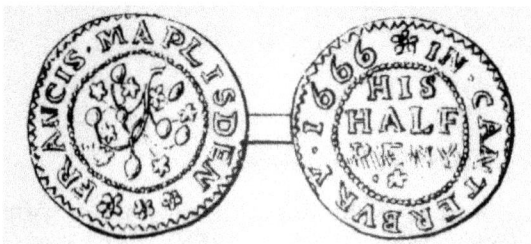

64. **O.** FRANCIS. MAPELSDAN = HIS HALF PENY. **R.** IN. CANTERBVRY. 1666 = A bunch of hops. (½)

Francis Maplisden was Mayor of Canterbury in 1668.

65. **O.** WALTER. MAPLISDEN = A dove with an olive-branch. **R.** IN. CANTERBVRY = W. S. M. (¼)

66. **O.** IEREMIAH. MASTERSON. AT = Checkers. **R.** = IN. CANTER-BERRY. HIS. HALF. PENNY. I. M. M (In seven lines). (*Octagonal*) (½)

The Chequers (of Hope) Inn stood on the corner of High Street and Mercery Lane. It was burnt down in 1865. The most interesting inn in Canterbury, also known by the name of Chaucer's Inn, it having been the lodging place of Chaucer and his band of pilgrims when visiting the shrine of St. Thomas à Becket in the cathedral. In 1475 Edward IV entertained the Earl of Essex, treasurer of England, and many noblemen and gentlemen at the Chequers.

67. **O.** THOMAS. MAYNE. GROCER = A Still. **R.** IN. CANTERBVRY. 1664 = HIS HALF PENY. (½)

68. **O.** THO. MAYNE. GROCER = A Still. **R.** IN. CANTERBVRY. 1654 = T. M. M. (¼)

590. **O.** THO. MAYNE. **R.** The Grocers' Arms. 164[?] (*In lead*) (¼)

69. **O.** THOMAS. OCKMAN = The arms of the Ockham family ; a fesse between three crescents. T. O. **R.** IN. CANTERBVRY = HIS HALF PENY. (½)

70. **O.** THOMAS. OCKMAN = The Ockham Arms. T. O. **R.** IN. CANTERBVRY = T. E. O. (¼)

Thomas Ockman was Mayor of Canterbury in 1658 and again in 1665.

71. **O.** THE. SARISONS. HEAD = A Saracen's head. **R.** IN. CANTERBVRY. 1653 = I. M. P. (¼)

72. **O.** AT. THE. MAIRMAYD = A mermaid. **R.** IN. CANTERBVRY = D. M. R. (¼)

The old inn was renamed the Music Hall Tavern and possibly stood in St Margaret's Street.

73. **O.** AT. THE. 3. MARRENORS = Three seamen standing. **R.** IN. CANTERBERY = T. M. S. (¼)

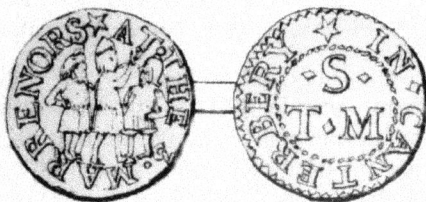

74. **O.** IOSEPH. SHERWOOD. IN = A woolpack. **R.** CANTERBVRY. GROCER = I. A. S. (¼)

75. **O.** IOHN. SIMPSON = A lion rampant. **R.** IN. CANTERBVRY. 1653 = I. I. S. (¼)

John Simpson was Mayor of Canterbury in 1667.

76. **O.** RICHARD. SMITH = The Grocers' Arms. **R.** IN. CANTERBVRY = R. E. S. (¼)

77. **O.** SIBB. SMITH. NEER = S. S. **R.** WEST. GATE. CANTERB = S. S. (¼)

78. A variety reads CANTERBVRY. (¼)

79. **O.** WILL. TERREY. AT. THE = A globe. **R.** GLOBE. IN. CANTERBVRYE = W. E. T. (¼)

80. **O.** AT. THE. 3. KINGS = The three magi. **R.** IN. CANTERBRY = E. A. W. (¼)

81. A variety has = E. M. W. (¼)

82. **O.** RICHARD. WHITE. BARBER = A Comb. **R.** IN. CANTERBVRY. 1656 = R. A. W. (¼)

83. **O.** IARVISE. WILLMATT = A horse. **R.** IN. CANTERBVRY. 1664 = HIS HALF PENY. (½)

84. A variety reads his HALFE PENY. (½)

CHARING

85. **O.** THOMAS. CHAPMAN. AT. YE. RED = A lion. **R.** AT. CHERING. HOTH. HIS. ½. PENY = T. F. C 1666. (½)

86. **O.** ALLEXANDER. HART. IN = The Grocers' Arms, A. H. **R.** CHARING. IN. KENT. GROCER = HIS HALF PENY. 1667. (½)

87. **O.** IOHN. MORS. IN = The Grocers' Arms. **R.** CHARING. IN. KENT. 1651 = I. M. M. (¼)

CHATHAM

88. **O.** IOHN. ADAMS. GVNER = A cannon mounted. **R.** IN. CHATHAM. 1657 = I. S. A. (¼)

88.1 **O.** ASHLY. BRETLIFFE = A ship. **R.** [IN. CHATHAM.] 1659 = A. A. B. (¼)

89. **O.** FRANCIS. BRETT = A comb. **R.** IN. CHATHAM. 1666 = F. S. B. (¼)

89.1. **O.** RICHARD. COTTAM = Three pipes. **R.** [IN. CHATHAM] 1657 = R. M. C. (¼)

90. **O.** RICHARD. CRESWELL = 1666. **R.** MEALMAN. IN. CHATHAM = R. H. C. (¼)

91. **O.** ROBERT. DIER. OF = HIS HALF PENY. R. I. D. **R.** CHATHAM. IN. KENT = A Catherine-wheel. (½)

92. **O.** WILLIAM. HARDIN. IN = Arms; three fishes. **R.** CHATTHAM. IN. KENT = W. A. H. (¼)

93. **O.** IOSHVA. HOLLAND = A cask. **R.** IN. CHATHAM. 1668 = l. M. H. (¼)

94. **O.** IOHN. IEFFERY = I. E. I. **R.** IN. CHATTHAM = A cheese-knife. (¼)

95. **O.** RICHARD. IEN. HIS. HALF = A horseshoe. **R.** PENNY. OF. CHETHAM. 1668 = R. E. I. (½)

96. **O.** RICHARD. IENNMAN = A bugle-horn. **R.** IN. CHATTHAM = R. P. I. (¼)

A tavern called the Trumpet stood at no. 60 High Street.

97. **O.** WALTER. IONES. AT. YE. NAGS. HED = A nag's head and bunch of grapes, W. I. I. **R.** TAVERNE. IN. CHATHAM = HIS HALFE PENNY. 1667. (½)

98. **O.** AT. THE. GLOBE. IN = A globe. **R.** CHATHAM. 1662 = W. S. I. (¼)

99. A variety is dated 1667. (¼)

The Globe was one of the principal hotels in Chatham.

100. **O.** IOHN. KNIGHT = A crown. **R.** IN. CHATHAM = I. O. K. (¼)

101. **O.** SAMVELL. MABB0R = The Grocers' Arms. **R.** IN. CHATAME. 1657 = S. S. M. (¼)

PAS LON-361CF5

102. **O.** IOHN. MARVELL = A frying-pan. **R.** IN. CHATHAM. 1666 = I. D. M. (¼)

103. **O.** RICHARD. MATHEWS = The Merchant-tailors' Arms. **R.** OF. CHATHAM. IN. KENT = R. M. M. (¼)

104. **O.** WALTER. RAMSDEN = A cannon mounted. **R.** LIVEING. AT. CHATTAM = An anchor. (¼)

105. **O.** AT. THE. GLOBE. IN = A globe. **R.** CHATHAM. 1657 = T. M. S. (¼)

106. **O.** FRANCIS. SANDERS = The Merchant-tailors' Arms. **R.** IN. CHATHAM = F. A. S. (¼)

107. **O.** ROBERT. SMITH. AT. YE. OLD = The King's Arms. **R.** KINGS. ARMES. 1671 = IN. CHATHAM. ½. (½)

108. **O.** ROBERT. SMITH. AT. YE. OLD = The King's Arms. **R.** IN. CHATHAM. 1671 = HIS HALF PENY. R. I. S. (½)

109. **O.** IOHN. TIHVRST. BREWER = The Brewers' Arms. **R.** IN. CHATTAM. 1666 = A Star with small star on the top point. I. T. (¼)

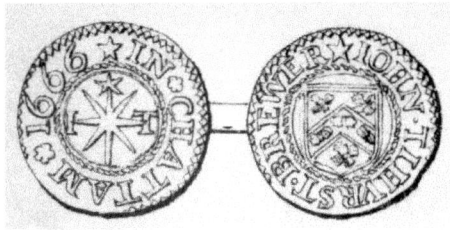

110. **O.** IOSEPH. WYMSHVRST = The Merchant-tailors' Arms. **R.** IN. CHATHAM. 1656 = I. M. W. (¼)

111. A variety has the reverse, IN. CHATTVM = I. M. W. (¼)

The names of Jeffery, Saunders, and Smith still occurred in Chatham at the end of the 19th century.

CHILHAM

112. **O.** IOHN. COLEMAN. 1664 = Arms; a chevron between three fleurs-de-lis. **R.** IN. CHILLOM. IN. KENT = HIS HALF PENY. (½)

The name of Coleman was still common in Chilham at the end of the 19th century.

113. **O.** IAMES. ODDEN. 1664 = The Grocers' Arms. **R.** IN. CHILLOM. IN. KENT = HIS HALF PENY. (½)

114. **O.** IAMES. ODDEN. 1659 = The Grocers' Arms. **R.** IN. CHILLOM. IN. KENT = I. O. (¼)

115. **O.** WILLIAM. PLVMER = The Grocers' Arms. **R.** OF. CHILHAM. IN. KENT = W. P. (¼)

COWDEN

116. **O.** IAM. IEANES. TALLOW = A stick of candles on a crescent moon, surrounded by seven stars. **R.** CHAN. IN. COVDEANE = I. M. I. (¼)

117. **O.** IOHN. OSBORNE = 1663. **R.** COWDEANE. MERCER = I. M. O. (¼)

117.1 **O.** IOHN. OSBVRNE = 1658. **R.** COWDEANE. MERCER = I. O. (¼)

PAS SUR-DF6B8C

CRANBROOK

118. **O.** IOHN. AVERY. OF = Three doves. **R.** CRANBROOKE. MER-CER = I. F. A. (¼)

The following; are extracts from the church register: 1656. October 2. A consent of marriage was published betweene John Avery, of Salehurste, in the county of Sussex, mercer, son of Thomas Avery, of Westfield, in the said county, yeoman, and Frances Turke, of Cranbrooke, in the county of Kent, spinster, daughter of Theophilus Turke, of Tenterden, in the said county, joyner; were married. — *Tho. Plvmer.*

The registers of burials are: 1678. November 7. John Avery. 1687. June 14. Frances Avery, vid[va].

119. **O.** THOMAS. BUTTERREY. OF = A man making candles. **R.** CRANBROOKE. MERCER = T. M. B. 1666. (¼)

120. **O.** THOMAS. DANIEL. OF = The Grocers' Arms. **R.** CRAN-BROCKE. IN. KENT = T. D. (¼)

The following are from the church registers: Marriages. — 1626. November 16. Thomas Daniell et Alice Monke. Buryalles. — 1658. September 7. Alis Monck, wife of Thomas Daniell of Cranbrooke Towne, mercer, and daughter of Jeffery Monck, sawyer. 1677. November 7. Thomas Daniell And only five days after: 1677. November 12. Sarah, wife of Thomas Danill.

Thomas Daniell was churchwarden of Cranbrook in 1660 and also in 1664.

121. **O.** RICH. FRANCKWELL = King's head with crown and sceptre. **R.** IN. CRAMBROOKE. 57 = R. E. F. (¼)

The following are from the church registers: Births. — 1653. February 13. Richard Frankwell, son of Richard Frankwell, vintner, and Elizabeth Adams, his wife. Buryalles. — 1653. May 6. Richard Frankwell, puer. Births. — 1656. July 13. Walter Frankwell, son of Richard Frankwell, vintner, and of Elizabeth Adams, his wife. Births. — 1660. June 3. Elizabeth Frankwell, daughter of Richard Frankwell, at the King's Head, vintner, and of Elizabeth Adams, uxor. Buryalles. — 1662. July 17. Elizabeth Franckwell, wife of Richard Frankwell and daughter of John Adams, of Chatton, innholder. Buryalles.— 1599. October 18. William Bettes, of Hide (Hythe), brooke his necke by a fall down a payer of stayers at the Kinge's Head. 1667. September 30. A stranger that died at the King's Head.

At the end of the 19th century this very old house was no longer a tavern, but still well-known, and turned into a draper's shop. An excellent open spring which supplied all the lower part of the town with water, was called King's Head Well, and was the property of that house.

121.1 **O.** G. K. = Lion and lamb. **R.** IN. CRANBROOKE. 1666 = G. C. K. (½)

122. **O.** THOMAS. MANDY = 1666. **R.** IN. CRANBROOKE = T. R. M. (¼)

Thomas Mandy contributed 6d towards the thirty thousand pounds required to recover English captives out of Turkish slavery. From the register: Buriall. — 1679. October 28. Thomas Mandy. "An affidavit was brought me 4th of November with a certificate that the said Thomas was buried in Woolen under the hands of Saml. Boys."

123. **O.** ROBERT. MARCH. OF = R. C. M. **R.** CRANBROCH. MERCER =1657. (¼)

The name of Robert March does not occur in the parish registers, but there are several entries with the same surname. Alexander, William, and Thomas March were sidesmen and overseers between the years 1617 and 1638.

124. **O.** PETER. MASTER. MERCER = The Grocers' Arms. **R.** CRANBROOCK. IN. KENT = P. A. M. (¼)

Among the parish registers only one is found containing the name of Master: Marriages. — 1665. June 5. A consent of marriage was published betweene Stephen South, of the parish of Saynt Mildred, in the city of Canterbury, cloth-worker; and Katherine Master, of Cranbrook, spinster. daughter of Peter Master, of this parish, mercer; were married before Thomas Plumer, Esquire, one of the justices of the peace of this county.

125. **O.** THOMAS. MVN. DRAPER = The Drapers' Arms. **R.** OF. CRANBROOCK. IN. KENT = T. M. M. (large ¼)

This was a large family in Cranbrook ; they filled the offices of sidesmen, overseers, and surveyors, and followed the trades of butchers, mercers, drapers, and broad-weavers. Of twenty-five entries of this family on the church registers three only appear to relate to the issuer of the token: Bury-alles. — 1691. March 27. Thomas Mann. 1691. July 23. Frances, daughter of Mary Mann. 1695. October 10. Mary Mann, widd.

126. **O.** IOHN. PARTON. IN. CRAN = HIS HALF PENY. **R.** BROOK. IN. KENT. 1669 = I. D. P. (½)

The following entries occur in the parish registers: Births. — 1668. October 27. Mary, daughter of John Parton, and Dorothy, his wife. 1673. May 26. Dorothy, daughter of John Parton, and Dorothy, his wife. And another daughter, Elizabeth, was baptized November 9, 1667. Buryalles. — 1676. August 24. John Parton.

127. **O.** WILLIAM. WACHER. IN = Three sugar-loaves. **R.** CRAN-BROOK. IN. KENT = W. M. W. (¼)

The issuer of this token was twice committed to Maidstone gaol for interrupting church services, and during his second imprisonment died there, after a confinement of ten weeks.

128. **O.** MARY. WILLIS. 1669 = The Pewterers' Arms. **R.** OF. CRAN-BROOCK = HER HALF PENY. I. M. W. (½)

Marriage. — 1661. September 16. John Willis, of Goudhurst, in the county of Kent, clothier, son of William Willis, of Tunbridge, husbandman, and Mary Merriam, of Goudhurst, in the county aforesaid, spinster, daughter of Thomas Merriam, of Goudhurst, in the county of Kent, husbandman, were maryed by William Goodrich, minister of Cranbrook parish— Goodrich was Presbyterian minister in the church during the Commonwealth. Buryall. — 1678. August 13. Mary Willis, widow.

We are indebted to William Tarbutt, Esq., of Cranbrook, for the whole of the notes on tokens of this town.

DARTFORD

130. **O.** ROBERT. CAPON. 1668 = The Tallowchandlers' Arms. **R.** IN. DARTFORD. IN. KENT = HIS HALF PENY. R. I. C (½)

There is no mention of Robert Capon in the registers, but the following entry occurs: Ann Capon was buried August 3, 1688.

131. **O.** NICHOLLAS. CHAMBERS = The Grocers' Arms. **R.** IN. DART-FORD. 1664 = N. M. C (¼)

His memorial in the north aisle of Dartford Church reads as follows: Nichollas Chambers, late of this parish, gent., dyed 11th October, in the year of our Lord 1685. On April 26, 1677, he was one who signed the churchwardens' accounts, and in several subsequent years. In 1685 was churchwarden, and died during his year of office.

132. **O.** THOMAS. GILL. OF = A hand holding scissors. **R.** DARTFORD. 1659 = T. A. G. (¼)

He was a tailor and cloth-merchant. During the Commonwealth and after the Restoration he filled some important positions in parish matters in Dartford. In 1652 he was one of the overseers. In 1660 was made one of the trustees of the grammar school. In 1662 was surveyor of highways, and in 1667 one of the churchwardens. In the churchwardens' accounts for the year 1660 there occurs the following entry: Pd. Thomas Gill for lining the pulpit-cloth 6s. 10d. He died in September,1667, whilst churchwarden.

133. **O.** ROBERT. GLOVER. OF = A bull. **R.** DARTFORD. IN. KENT = R. I. G. (¼)

He was a vintner, and his name occurs in a deed or lease dated 1660, under which himself and nineteen other inhabitants of Dartford hold some church lands. In all probability Robert Glover kept the old Bull at Dartford, an ancient inn, still existing as The Royal Victoria and Bull Hotel, and a noted house in the old coaching days.

134. **O.** WILLIAM. HVISH = A cock. **R.** DERTFORD. IN. KENT = W. A. H. (¼)

He was one who signed the churchwardens' accounts on "May, ye 18th, 1663, for ye year ending Lady-day" and was churchwarden in 1679.

135. **O.** ISAAC. MANNING. 1664 = Arms of the Manning family; a cross fleury between four trefoils. **R.** OF. DARTFORD. IN. KENT = HIS FAR-THING. (Large ¼)

The only entry in the Dartford register relating to this issuer is as follows: A child of Isaac Manning buried 20th August, 1666.

136. **O.** THO. MORLEY. AT. YE. HORSHO = A horse-shoe. **R.** AT. DARFORD. IN. KENT = HIS HALFE PENY. (½)

137. **O.** HENRY. PEIRCE. OF = A sugar-loaf. **R.** DERTFORD. IN. KENT = H. P. (¼)

138. A variety has on the reverse the initials H. M. P. (¼)

He was a grocer, and one of those who signed the churchwardens' accounts in 1679. In 1680 and in 1681 he was one of the churchwardens.

139. **O.** WILLIAM. PHILLIPES = A stick of candles within a crescent. **R.** IN. DARTFORD. IN. KENT = W. S. P. (¼)

140. **O.** EDWARD. ROSE. OF = A rose. **R.** DARFORD. IN. KENT = E. M. R. (¼)

He was a yeoman, and is so described in the deed which he, in conjunction with Robert Glover and others, signed in 1660.

141. **O.** REBECKA. SMITH = R. S. **R.** IN. DERFORDE = The Butchers' Arms. (¼)

142. **O.** THOMAS. SMITH = A crown. **R.** DERTFORD. IN. KENT = T. M. S. (¼)

143. **O.** ROBERT. TAYLOR = A falcon. **R.** IN. DARTFORD. 1667 = HIS HALF PENY. (½)

The notes on the issuers of Dartford tokens were kindly contributed from parochial papers, etc., by H. W. Smith, Esq., of Belvedere.

DEAL

144. **O.** THOMAS. BROTHERS = A pair of scales. **R.** OF. DEALE. 1664 = T. A. B. (¼)

145. **O.** WILLIAM. BROTHERS = HIS HALF PENY. **R.** IN. DEALE. 1669 = A ship. (½)

146. **O.** ANN. CAVTEREL = A pair of scales. **R.** OF. DEALE. 1669 = HER HALF PENY. (½)

147. **O.** IOHN. CLARKE = A man and still. **R.** IN. DEALE. 1659 = I. M. C. (¼)

148. **O.** IAMES. COSTON = I. E. C. and a heart. **R.** OF. DEALL. 1653 = I. E. C. and a heart. (¼)

PAS IOW-E318B3

149. A variety reads DEALE. (¼)

150. **O.** WILLIAM. COVLSON = An eagle and child. **R.** IN. DEALL. 1659 = W. I. C. (¼)

151. **O.** AT. THE. DOLPHINE = A dolphin. **R.** IN. DEALE. 1658 = T. F. (¼)

This tavern is not remembered in Deal; it was evidently situated in the street now called Dolphin Street.

152. **O.** TIMOTHY. GARDNER = Arms; a chevron ermine between three griffins' heads ; impaling, a chevron ermine between three demi-lions. **R.** IN. DEALE. 1666 = T. S. G. (¼)

153. **O.** IOHN. LOBDELL. IN. DEALE = A pair of scissors. **R.** HIS. HALF. PENY. 1669 = I. I. L. (¼)

154. **O.** THOMAS. PARKSOEN = The Grocers' Arms. **R.** IN. DELL. 1658 = T. R. P. (¼)

155. **O.** IOHN. PEARS. IN = A heart. **R.** DEALE. 1663 = I. I. P. (¼)

156. **O.** IOHN. PITTOCK = A hand. **R.** IN. DEALL. 1656 = I. E. P. (¼)

157. **O.** WILLIAM. PITTOCKE. IN = D. Y. Bust of the Duke of York. **R.** DEALE. HIS. HALFE. PENNY = W. P. 1668. (½)

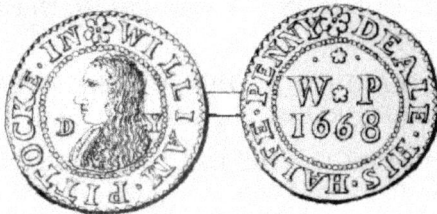

158. **O.** MOYSES. POTTER. AT = The Bakers' Arms. **R.** DEALE. IN. KENT = M. P. (¼)

159. **O.** THOMAS. POTTER = The Grocers' Arms. **R.** IN. DEALE. 1663 = T. M. P. (¼)

160. **O.** RICHARD. STVTLY = R. M. S. **R.** IN. DELL. 1653 = R. M. S. (¼)

161. **O.** PETER. VNDERWOOD = A man making candles. **R.** IN. LOWER. DEALL = P. E. V. (¼)

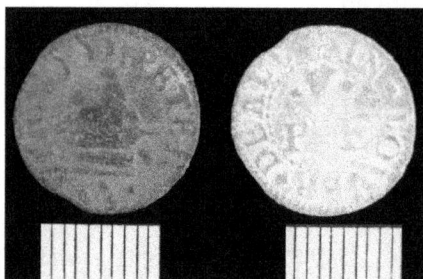

PAS KENT-9475A0

162. **O.** IOHN. WATTS. OF = A fleece. **R.** DEALE. 1664 = I. M. W. (¼)

At the end of the 19th century the names of Brothers and Pittock were still to be found in Deal.

DEPTFORD.

163. **O.** IOHN. ANDREWS = A globe. **R.** IN. DEDFORD. 1655 = I. I. A. (¼)

164. **O.** WILLIAM. ARCHER = An archer. **R.** IN. DEPTFORD. 1665 = HIS HALFE PENY. (½)

165. **O.** THOMAS. BRIOND. IN = The Bakers' Arms. **R.** DEPTHFORD. 1665 = T. R. B. (¼)

166. **O.** GREGORY. BVMPSTED = A Catherine-wheel. **R.** IN. DEPT-FORD. 1656 = G. E. B. (¼)

167. **O.** THOMAS. CHILD. IN = A sugar-loaf. **R.** DEPTFORD. CHAN-DLER = T. B. C. (¼)

168. **O.** ROGER. CLARKE. AT. THE = HIS HALF PENY. **R.** ROYAL. OAKE. IN. DEPFORD = R. E. C. (½)

169. **O.** WILLIAM. CRICH = HIS HALF PENY. **R.** IN. DEPTFORD = The Grocers' Arms. (½)

170. **O.** WILLIAM. CRICH = The Grocers' Arms. **R.** IN. DEPTFORD = W. S. C. 1663. (¼)

171. **O.** IOHN. CROVCH. 1658 = A wheatsheaf. **R.** IN. DEPTFORD = I. A. C. (¼)

172. **O.** WILLAM. DRING = W. V. D. **R.** IN. DEPTFORD. 1651 = W. V. D. (¼)

173. **O.** MARGERY. FVRZER = 1667. **R.** IN. DEDFORD = HIR HALF PENY. (½)

174. **O.** GEORGE. GORHAM = G. A. G. in monogram. **R.** IN. DEPTFORD. 1665 = HIS HALF PENY. (½)

175. **O.** GEORGE. GORHAM. 1664. **R.** IN. DEDFORD = G. A. G in monogram. (¼)

176. **O.** IOHN. HODGES. AT. THE = Three goats' heads. **R.** 3. GOAT. HEAD. IN. DEPFORD = I. H. (¼)

177. **O.** IOHN. HODGES. IN = I. B. H. **R.** LOWER. DEDFORD = I. B. H. (¼)

178. **O.** IOHN. HOMES. AT. THE = A large ball. **R.** BALL. IN. DEPTFORD = I. S. H. (¼)

179. **O.** IOHN. HORLOK. AT. THE = A lion rampant. **R.** RED. LYON. IN. DEPFORD = I. H. (¼)

180. **O.** RICHARD. IEFRY. IN = R. S. I. **R.** DEPTFORD. MEALL MAN = R. S. I. (¼)

181. **O.** MATHEW. IESSON. AT. THE = A lion rampant. **R.** WHIT. LYON. IN. DEPFORD = M. I. (¼)

182. **O.** IOHN. KERBEY = HIS HALF PENY. **R.** IN. DEPTFORDE = A sugar-loaf. (½)

183. **O.** AT. THE. KINGS. HEAD = Head of James I, crowned. **R.** IN. DEPTFORD. 1648 = N. D. L. (¼)

184. Another, similar, dated 1649. (¼)

The King's Head stood at 199 Church Street and has now been demolished.

185. **O.** IOHN. LINES. 1668 = The Weavers' Arms. **R.** IN. DEPTHFORD = I. C. L. (½)

186. **O.** RICHARD. MANSFEILD = HIS HALFE PENY. **R.** IN. DEAD-FORD. 1665 = R. M. (½)

187. **O.** ANTHONY. MATHEWS. AT. YE = A roll of tobacco. **R.** IN. DETFORD. 1659 = A. M. M. (¼)

188. **O.** PETER. PEMELL = A Castle. **R.** AT. DEPTFORD. 1666 = P. M. P. (¼)

189. **O.** AT. THE. KINGS. HEAD = Head of James I, crowned. **R.** IN. DEPTHFORD. 1657 = M. A. R. (¼)

190. **O.** IOHN. SMITH = HIS HALF PENY. **R.** IN. DEPTHFORD = The Weavers' Arms. (½)

191. **O.** WILLIAM. STONE = W. A. S. **R.** IN. DEPTFORD. 1652 = W. A. S. (¼)

192. **O.** EDWARD. SWALLOW = A talbot passant. **R.** IN. LOER. DEPTFORD = E. A. S. 1656. (¼)

193 A variety is dated 1658. (¼)

194. **O.** IOHN. WALLIS. AT. THE. BLEW = A wild boar. **R.** BORE. IN. DEDFORD. 1668 = HIS HALFE PENNY. I. M. W. (½)

195. **O.** IAMES. WATTERS. IN = HIS HALF PENY. **R.** DEPTFORD. MEALMAN = A pair of scales. (½)

196. **O.** ISAAC. WELCH = A lion rampant in a shield. **R.** IN. DEPT-FORD. 1664 = I. E. W. (¼)

DODDINGTON

196.1 **O.** RICHARD. NIN = A pair of scales. ½D. **R.** OF DVDINGTON = R. N. (½)

DYMCHURCH

197. **O.** ANDREW. CLIFFORD. BLACK = An anvil. **R.** SMITH. IN. DIMCHVRCH. KENT = HIS HALF PENY. A. S. C. (½)

From the Dymchurch registers we learn that Andrew Clifford married Sarah Hoad, a widow, April 14, 1670, and that he was buried November 18, 1672.

DOVER

198. **O.** FOR. THE. POORE. OF. DOVER = St Martin on horse-back, dividing his cloak with a beggar, who is following him. **R.** A. HALFE. PENNY. 1668 = Arms of Dover; three demi-lions, impaling three demi-hulks. (½)

199. **O.** DOVER. FARTHING. 68 = Arms of Dover. **R.** (No legend) = St. Martin and a beggar. (¼)

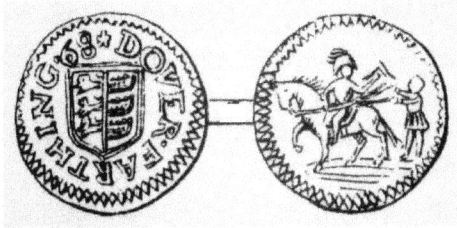

St Martin in Roman Catholic times was patron-saint of Dover and the church of St. Martin-Le-Grand the mother-church. Amongst its other privileges was that of beginning service before all the other churches and chapels in the district. The church was destroyed at the time of the Reformation. Dover Fair was called St. Martin's Fair.

The same device as on the tokens appears on the borough counter-seal, which dates as far back as the year 1305. This has been described by Browne Willis as: "a highwayman robbing a man on foot." The obverse side of the seal has an antique ship with sail furled, a forecastle, poop, and round-top all embattled; a steersman at the helm, two men on the forecastle blowing horns, another climbing up the shrouds, two below at a rope; a flag at the stern charged with the port arms. It is an admirable specimen of engraving for the period.

The following minutes are from the corporation records of Dover, 1667 and 1668: It is ordered and decreed that a certain quantity of farthings and halfpence be provided and stamped by the corporation, for the use of the overseers of the poor and others; and to be stamped in a manner and form as shall be advised and directed by Mr. Mayor, Mr. John Golder, Mr. George West, Mr. John Carlisle, Mr. William Pepper, Mr. John Matson, Mr. Richard Barley, jurats; the chamberlains for the time being Warren Hugeson, and Bartholomew Anderson; or as any five or more of them shall think fit, upon the account of this corporation. Examined, Alexander Wellarde, Common Clerke. Dover. At a common assembly holden the 30th day of March, 1668: Whereas according to a late decree, there is provided and put into the chamberlains' hands the value of 32 lb., or thereabouts, in farthings and halfpence, for the use of the corporation; it is thought fit and so ordered that the chamberlains do, upon all occasions, exchange so many of them, as hath or shall, at any time hereafter, be delivered out to any person or persons whatsoever of the said town and port. Examined, Alexander Wellarde, Common Clerk.

200. **O.** DAVID. ADAMSON = An anchor. **R.** IN. DOVER. 1657 = D. M. A. (¼)

201. **O.** AT. THE. SKOCH. ARMES = An unicorn. **R.** IN. DOVER. 1658 = I. A. B. (¼)

202. **O.** JOHN. BRIAN = I. S. B. **R.** IN. DOVER. 1652 = I. S. B. (¼)

203. **O.** AT. THE. QVEENE. OF = Her bust, full-faced. **R.** BOHEMIA. IN. DOVER = I. M. C. (¼)

204. **O.** AT. THE. GEORGE = St. George and the dragon. **R.** IN. DOVER. 1652 = I. E. C. (¼)

205. **O.** EDWARD. CHAMBERS = The Grocers' Arms. **R.** IN. DOVER. 1649 = E. E. C. (¼)

206. **O.** IANE. COLLER = I. C. **R.** IN. DOVER = I. C. (¼)

207. **O.** RICHARD. COOKE. IN = A shovel. R. C. **R.** DOVER. SEIGNIOR = HIS HALFE PENY. 1669. (½)

208. **O.** RICHARD. CULLEN = The Grocers' Arms. **R.** GROCER. IN. DOVER. 1656 = R. F. C. A merchant' s mark. (¼)

Richard Cullen, by will, in 1696, gave a house and land, the yearly income be distributed every Sunday evening to twenty poor widows of St. Mary's, Dover. He likewise gave another small cottage, the rent of it to be distributed in bread.

209. **O.** AT. THE. LEOPOVLDVS = The Emperor's bust, and a crown. **R.** IN. DOVER. 1651 = C. M. D. (¼)

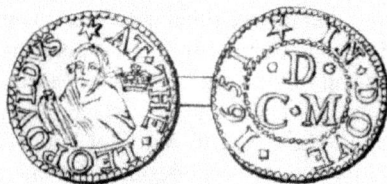

210. **O.** A variety reads LEOPVLDVS. (¼)

211. **O.** AT. THE. LEOPVLDVS = The Emperor's bust. **R.** IN. DOVER. 1666 = G. M. F. (¼)

212. **O.** MARTHA. FFORD = M. F. **R.** IN. DOVAR. 1659 = M. F. (¼)

213. **O.** THOMAS. FIDG. AT. THE = The Mercers' Arms. **R.** MAYDEN. HEAD. IN. DOVER = T. M. F. (¼)

PAS LON-7911B3

214. **O.** ROBART. GALLANT. AT. THE = A horse prancing. **R.** WHITE. HORSE. IN. DOVER = R. G. (¼)

The White Horse Inn is still standing.

215. **O.** KATHEREN. GARDNER = DOVER. K. G. **R.** IN. DOVER. CHANLER. 1667= HER HALFE PENNY. (½)

216. **O.** KATHEREN. GARDNER = DOVER. K. G. **R.** IN. DOVER. 1667 = CHANLER. (¼)

217. **O.** THOMAS. GREEN. OF. DOVER = A rose. **R.** HIS. HALFE. PENNY. 1666 = T. M. G. (½)

218. **O.** IOHN. HALL = 1666. **R.** IN. DOVER = I. R. H. (¼)

219. **O.** IOHN. HAYNES. BAKER = The Bakers' Arms. **R.** IN. DOVER. 1655 = I. E. H. (¼)

220. **O.** IAMES. HOMARD = The Bakers' Arms. **R.** BAKER. IN. DO-VER = I. E. H. (¼)

221. **O.** WILLIAN. KEYLOCKE = The Goldsmiths' Arms. **R.** IN. DO-VER. 1667 =W. M. K. (¼)

222. **O.** PINES. KITE = The Bakers' Arms. **R.** IN. DOVER. 1670 = HIS HALF PENY. P. M. K. (½)

223. **O.** THO. KITE. IN = A boat rigged. **R.** DOVER. 1656 = T. M. K. (¼)

224. **O.** AT. THE. FRENCH = The Arms of France, crowned. **R.** ARMES. IN. DOVER = D. M. N. (¼)

225. **O.** IOHN. PARKER = Three doves. **R.** AT. THE. PEERE. IN. DO-VER = I. P. (¼)

226. **O.** SAMVEL. PARTRICH = S. M. P. **R.** MILLENER. OF. DOVER = S. M. P. (¼)

227. **O.** THOMAS. PIEARCE. IVNIOR = The Tallowchandlers' Arms. **R.** OF. DOVER. 1669 = HIS DVBBLE TOKEN. (½)

228. **O.** ROGER. ROGERS = A greyhound. **R.** IN. DOVER. 1665 = R. F. R. (¼)

229. **O.** SUSAN. SHARNALL = S. S. **R.** OF. DOVER. 1656 = S. S. (¼)

230. **O.** THOMAS. SHARNAL = 1658. **R.** IN. DOVER = T. E. S. (¼)

231. **O.** THOMAS. STIVEDAY = T. I. S. **R.** IN. DOVER. 1653 = T. I. S. (¼)

232. **O.** SARAH. SWEETLAND = A pair of scales. **R.** IN. DOVER. 1658 = S. S.

233. **O.** SAMVELL. TAVENOR = Arms of the Tavenor family; argent, a bend lozengy, sable ; in sinister chief, a torteau. **R.** OF. DOVER. 1669 = S. S. T. HIS HALF PENY. (½)

234. **O.** IOHN. THOMAS = Three horse-shoes. **R.** GROCER. IN. DOVER = I. A. T. (¼)

235. **O.** WILLIAM. TILLIT = The Coopers' Arms. **R.** IN. DOVER = W. M. T. (¼)

236. A variety is dated 1662 on reverse. (¼)

237. **O.** MARY. TVRK. 1659 = The Grocers' Arms. **R.** IN. DOVER. GROSER = M. T. (¼)

238. **O.** WIL. WARDEN. AT. THE. HORS = A horse prancing. **R.** AND. HORS. SHOOE. IN. DOVER = W. M. W. A horse-shoe. (¼)

239. **O.** WILL. WELLARD. AT = A rose. **R.** THE. COCK. IN. DOVER = W. A. W. (¼)

240. **O.** ROBERT. WOODGREEN = A rose. **R.** IN. DOVER. 1666 = R. E. W. (¼)

241. **O.** ROBART. WOODGREEN = R. E. W. **R.** OF. DOVER. 1658 = R. E. W. (¼)

At the end of the 19th century the following names were still to be found in Dover: Collier, Cooke, Cullen, Gardener, Green, Hall, Kite, and Tavenor.

EASTCHURCH

242. **O.** RICHARD. EAGLESTON = The Blacksmiths' Arms. **R.** IN. EASTCHVRCH. 1665 = HIS HALFE PENY. (½)

243. **O.** WILL. MANYARINGE. OF. EST. CHVRCH = D. Y. Bust of the Duke of York. **R.** IN. YE. ILE. OF. SHEPWAY. HABERDASHER = HIS HALF PENY. (½)

244. A variety reads MANYRINGE. (½)

EDENBRIDGE

245. **O.** ROB. ALCHORNE. WIL. ABLET. AT = THER HALF PENY. **R.** EATON. BRIDG. IN. KENT. MERCERS = The Mercers'Arms. (½)

246. **O.** KATHERINE. HVBERD. OF = A crown. **R.** EATTON. BRIDGE. IN. KENT = HER HALFE PENY. (½)

ELHAM

246.1. **O.** IOHN FORMAN 1664 = The Grocers' Arms. **R.** OF. ELHAM = acorn and oak spray. (¼)

247. **O.** WILLIAM. PARTRIDGE = The Grocers' Arms. **R.** OF. ELE-HAM. HIS. ½ = W. P. (½)

248. **O.** WILLIAM. PARTRIDG = The Grocers' Arms. **R.** OF. ELHAM = W. P. (¼)

249. **O.** RICHARD. SYMONS. OF = The Grocers' Arms. **R.** ELHAM. IN. KENT. GROCER = R.M.S. 1664. (¼)

ELTHAM

250. **O.** IOHN. BLANDEN. OF = A measure. **R.** ELLTHAM. MALTMAN = I. I. B. (¼)

251. **O.** RICHARD. GREENE. IN = The Carpenters' Arms. **R.** ELTHOM. IN. KENT. 1667 = R. I. G. (¼)

At the end of the 19th century the Green family was still at Eltham.

252. **O.** THE. CASTELL. TAVERNE = A castle. **R.** IN. ELTHAM. 1649 = N. T. M. (¼)

At the end of the 19th century the old house was still standing in almost its original state.

ERITH

253. **O.** ROBERT. DVTTON. 1667 = R. M. D. **R.** OF. ERITH. IN. KENT = HIS HALFE PENNY. (½)

255. **O.** BRYAN. RVSSELL. OF = 1671. **R.** ERITH. IN. KENT = B. M. R. (¼)

256. **O.** FRANCIS. TAYLOR = A crown and fleur-de-lis. **R.** TVRNSTYLE. ERITH = F. A. T. (¼)

257. **O.** COVLLVERWELL = C. M. T. **R.** TOLLVER. AT. ERITH = C. M. T. (¼)

258. **O.** ROB. TOY. 1666 = A hen and chickens. **R.** IN. EARRIFE= R. S. T. (¼)

259. **O.** AT. THE. COCKE = A Cock. **R.** IN. EREFE = R. K. W. (¼)

EYNESFORD

260. **O.** IOHN. BECKET. 1658. OF = The Grocers' Arms. **R.** AINES-FORD. IN. KENT = I. E. B. (¼)

FARNBOROUGH

261. **O.** WILLIAM. BEST. AT. THE = St George and dragon. **R.** IN. FARNBOROGH. 1668 = HIS HALF PENY. (½)

FARNINGHAM

262. **O.** HENRY. POVND. 1658. IN = The Grocers' Arms. **R.** FARING-HAM. IN. KENT = H. P. (¼)

FAVERSHAM

263. **O.** GEORGE. ALLEN. 1666 = A horse-shoe. **R.** IN. FEAVERSHAM = HIS HALF PENY. (½)

George Allen was Mayor of Faversham in 1680.

264. **O.** IOHN. BEALE. MERCER = The Mercers' Arms. **R.** IN. FEVER-SHAM. 1649 = The Grocers' Arms. (¼)

265. A variety reads BELE. (¼)

266. **O.** WILLIAM. BVCK. 1669 = A Stag Standing. **R.** IN. FEVER-SHAM = HIS HALF PENY. (½)

The bearers of this name were a considerable family in Faversham; but had disappeared by the end of the 19th century.

267. **O.** PHILLIP. BVTLER = A crown under a rainbow. **R.** OF. FEVER-SHAM. HIS. HALF. PENNY. 1669 (in five lines). (*Square.*) (½)

The wife of Philip Butler was buried in Faversham Church, 1676.

268. **O.** AT. THE. QVEENE. ARMES = Arms; France and England quarterly. **R.** IN. FAVERSHAM. 1651 = R. E. C. (¼)

269. **O.** IOHN. CLEARE. 1666 = A crown. **R.** OF. FEAVERSHAM = HIS HALF PENY. (½)

270. **O.** IOHN. ELLIS. BACKER = HIS HALFE PENY. **R.** IN. FE-
VERSVM. 1667 = A wheatsheaf. (½)

Jacobs, in his **History of Faversham**, 1774, mentions that tokens were
issued by the common porters deputy, the backer (or carrier) of corn from
the quays to the vessels in the creek.

271. **O.** ROBERT. HOGBEN = The Vintners' Arms. **R.** IN. FEVER-
SHAM = HIS HALF PENY. (½)

The Three Tuns, one of the oldest taverns in Faversham, is still standing,
and the name of Hogben is common among the present inhabitants.

272. **O.** WILLIAM. KNIGHT. 1666 = The Grocers' Arms. W. I. K. **R.** IN.
FEAVERSHAM = HIS HALF PENY. (½)

273. **O.** IAMES. MARCH. 1669 = The Grocers' Arms. **R.** IN. FEVER-
SHAM. IN. KENT = HIS HALF PENY. I. A. M. (½)

274. **O.** POARE. NED. 1667 = HIS HALF PENY. **R.** IN. FEVERSHAM.
IN. KENT = A tree. (½)

Ned was probably a gardener; indicated by his device, a tree— the cherry-
tree — still extensively cultivated in this part of the country.

275. **O.** IOHN. PIEARCE. IN. FEVERSHAM. 1667 (in five lines). **R.**
HIS. HALF. PENNY = A dolphin. (*Octagonal*) (½)

At the end of the 19th century, the old house in Preston Street was still
named The Dolphin, and ranked as the second tavern in Faversham. It was
demolished in 1960.

276. **O.** ROBERT. PRESTON = HIS HALF PENY. **R.** IN. FEVRSHAM.
1664 = THE QVEENS ARMES. (½)

The Queen's Arms had a distinguished, though unwilling visitor, in the
year 1688, when James II. was intercepted in his endeavour to leave the
country, and was brought into Faversham by some sailors of the town.

277. **O.** FRANCIS. WATERMAN = The Mercers' Arms. **R.** IN. FAVE-
SHAM = F. S. W. (¼)

He was mayor in 1665 and again in 1681. Sarah, wife of Francis Waterman, was buried in Faversham Church, 1694, and Francis himself in 1707.

FOLKESTONE

278. **O.** EDWARD. FRANKLIN = HIS HALF PENY. **R.** OF.
FOVLSTON. IN. KENT = E. E. F. 70. (½)

279. **O.** EDWARD. FRANKLING = HIS HALF PENY. **R.** OF.
FOVLTON. IN. KENT = E. E. F. (½)

FOOTS CRAY

280. **O.** IOHN. MOORE. AT. THE = A griffin's head. **R.** IN. FVTSCRAY. 1668 = HIS HALF PENY. (½)

281. **O.** MICHAELL. PITMAN = The Brewers' Arms. **R.** FOOTES. CRAY. IN. KENT = M. E. P. (¼)

GILLINGHAM

282. **O.** WILLIAM. COLES. HALF. PENY = The Carpenters' Arms. **R.** AT. GILINGAME. FOORT. 1669 = A malt-shovel (½)

GODMERSHAM

283. **O.** ROBERT. OAKLEY. OF = HIS HALF PENY. **R.** GOD-MASHAM. IN. KENT = The Grocers' Arms. (½)

GOUDHURST

284. **O.** IOHN. AVSTEN. OF = The Mercers' Arms. **R.** GOVTHERST. MERCER = I. B. A. (¼)

285. **O.** WILLIAM. MAYNARD. OF = 1664. **R.** GOODHVRST. IN. KENT. MERC = W. M. M. (¼)

285.1 **O.** RICHARD PVXTY. AT THE = The Grocers' Arms. **R.** IN GOODHVRST. IN. KENT. = HIS HALF PENY. (½)

285.2 **O.** RICHARD PVXTY. AT THE = The Grocers' Arms. **R.** IN GOODHVRST. IN. KENT. = 1669 R. M. P. (½)

286. **O.** = S. H. S. STEPHEN. STRINGER 1661 (in five lines). **R.** OF. GOWDHAST. IN. KENT = An anchor with s on it, to the left II. (½)

287. **O.** = S. H. S STEPHEN. STRINGER. 1661 (in five lines). **R.** GOWDHAST. IN. KENT = An anchor with s on it, to the left I. (¼)

Stephen Stringer placed the value on his tokens, II representing two and I, one farthing.

GRAVESEND

288. **O.** IOHN. BIDDLE = A Pope's head. **R.** IN. GRAVESEND. 1670 = HIS HALF PENY. (½)

289. **O.** MARGRET. BIRD = A hen and chickens. **R.** AT. GRAVESEND.
1657 = M. B. (¼)

Margaret Bird was probably widow of a Gravesend publican, whose tavern
with another was pulled down by order of the Council of State, in 1649; by
reason that much injury was done the Commonwealth by illegally shipping
gold and silver and conveying away and receiving letters of dangerous
consequence to and from disaffected persons, from these taverns.

290. **O.** THOMAS. BOONE = A roll of tobacco. **R.** IN. GRAVESEND =
T. M. B. (¼)

291. **O.** *Matthew Butler in Graves end* (in four lines). **R.** *His HalfePeny*
1668. M. B. B. (in five lines) (*Octagonal*) (½)

292. **O.** IOHN. CHEESMAN. AT. THE = The sun in splendour. **R.** SVN.
IN. GRAVESEND = I. E. C. (¼)

293. **O.** THOMAS. CLARKE. AT. BORES = A boar's head. **R.** HAD. IN. GRAVESEND = T. M. C. (¼)

293.1 **O.** THOMAS. CLARKE. AT. BORES = A boar's head, with apple in mouth. **R.** HAD. IN. GRAVESEND = T. M. C. (¼)

294. **O.** WILLIAM. CROVCH = A hand holding a bird. **R.** IN. GRAVSEND. 1658 = W. C. (¼)

295. **O.** ROBERT. DAY. SHOPKEEPER = A pair of scissors. **R.** IN. GRAVESEND. 1667 = HIS HALF PENY. (½)

Robert Day was a Quaker. He was imprisoned in Maidstone gaol on account of his religious opinions.

296. **O.** THOMAS. HILL. GROCER = The Grocers' Arms. **R.** OF. GRAVESEND = T. S. H. (¼)

296.1 A variety dated 1651 = T. S. H. *(In lead)* (¼)

297. **O.** IOHN. MAY. 1666 = St Christopher with a staff carrying Jesus **R.** IN. GRAVESEND = I. A. M. (¼)

298. **O.** MARCK. MEDHOVST. IN = HIS HALF PENY. **R.** GRAVES END. MERCER = M. M. M. (½)

299. **O.** WILLIAM. OLIVER. AT = A cannon mounted. **R.** IN. GRAVES-END = W. M. O. (¼)

300. **O.** AT. THE. MAREMAID. IN = A mermaid. **R.** GRAVESEND. 1655 = I. D. P. (¼)

301. **O.** IACOB. PARSON = Two hands joined. **R.** IN. GRAVES END. 1651 = I. E. P. (¼)

302. A variety has the name spelled PARSSON. (¼)

Jacob Parson was Mayor of Gravesend in 1656, and again in 1668.

303. **O.** IOH. PIKE. AT. BLACK = An anchor. **R.** ANKER. IN. GRAVE-SED = I. M. P. (¼)

304. **O.** IOHN. REDDELL = An anchor. **R.** IN. GRAVESEND = I. E. R. (¼)

305. **O.** IOHN. REDDELL = The King's head crowned **R.** IN. GRAVES-END = I. E. R. (¼)

John Reddell was Mayor in 1660, during the year of the restoration of Charles II. When the King's arms were painted and set up in the town hall, his name was painted on the frame, where it remains.

306. **O.** AT. THE. SWANE = A swan. **R.** IN. GRAVESEND = A. M. W. (¼)

307. **O.** THOMAS. WARREN = Three rabbits. **R.** IN. GRAVES END. 1671 = T. I. W. (¼)

308. **O.** IOHN. WATSON = A heart pierced with an arrow **R.** IN. GRAWSEND. 1653 = I. K. W. (¼)

He was mayor in 1660, and again in 1670.

309. **O.** IOHN. WETSON = A Toll of tobacco. **R.** IN. GRAVES. END = I. K. W. (¼)

310. **O.** THOMAS. WOOD. OF = T. E. W. and a heart **R.** GRAVSEND. 1657 = T. E. W. and a heart (¼)

GREENHITHE

311. **O.** WILLIAM. CHATTWIN = The Tallowchandlers' Arms. **R.** OF. GREENEHIVE. KENT = W. C. (¼)

312. **O.** RICHARD. SMITH = A goat's head and shoemaker's knife. **R.** IN. GREENEHIVE. KENT = R. S. S. (¼)

GREENWICH

313. **O.** = THOMAS. ANDREY. GREENWICH. 1668. T. A. E. (in five lines). **R.** HIS. HALFE. PENNY = The Joiners' Arms. (*Octagonal*) (½)

314. **O.** AT. THE. GEORGE = St. George and the dragon. **R.** IN. GREENWICH = E. B. (¼)

315. A variety reads GREENEWICH. (¼)

316. Another variety reads GRENEWICH. (¼)

317. Another reads GORGE on obverse, and GRENEWICH on reverse. (¼)

318. **O.** EDWARD. BARTLETT = A hart lodged. **R.** IN. GREENWICH = E. M. B. (¼)

319. **O.** HENREY. BEDBERY. ROSE = A rose. **R.** IN. EAST. GREEN-WICH = H. R. B. (¼)

320. **O.** WILLIAM. CLEARE = A wheatsheaf. **R.** OF. GREENEWICH = W. M. C. (¼)

321. **O.** THOMAS. COLTON = The Mercers' Arms. **R.** IN. GREEN-WICH. 1667 = HIS HALF PENY. (½)

322. **O.** WILLIAM. DISKETT = A roll of tobacco. **R.** IN. GRENWICH. 1659 = W. S. D. (¼)

323. **O.** ALEX. DRIVER. SILK = Arms. **R.** THROSTER. IN. GRIN-WICH = A. A. D. (¼)

324. **O.** ADAM. EDGHELL. AT. YE. 3 = Three fleurs-de-lis. **R.** IN. GREENWICH. 1667 = HIS HALFE PENY. (½)

325. **O.** IOHN. ELLIS = A sugar-loaf. **R.** IN. GRENEWICH = I. H. E. (¼)

326. **O.** THOMAS. FOSTER. AT. THE = A nag's head. **R.** IN. GREEN-WICH. 1667 = HIS HALF PENY. T. E. F. (½)

327. **O.** HENRY. GIPPES = A pot of lilies. **R.** AT. GRINWICH. 1668 = HIS HALFE PENNY. (½)

328. **O.** ROBERT. GIRDIS. IN. YE. OVLD = R. M. G. **R.** BEARE. YARD. IN. GREENWICH = HIS HALF PENY. (½)

329. **O.** WILLIAM. LEE. IN. GRINWICH = The Brewers' Arms. **R.** HIS. HALFE. PENNY. 1666. W. F. L. (½)

330. **O.** RICHARD. [or ROBERT] MILINGTON = The Ironmongers' Arms. **R.** GREENWICH. IRONMONGER = 1663. (¼)

331. **O.** AT. THE. BARE. TAVERNE = A bear with chain. **R.** IN. GREENWICH. 1650 = E. E. P. (¼)

332. **O.** ROBERT. POLADAYE. AT. THE = A still **R.** IN. GREEN-WICH. 1667 = HIS HALF PENY. R. M. P. (½)

333. **O.** HVGH , PVDEFOVRD. AT. THE = A horse. **R.** WHITE. HORSE. IN. GREENWICH = HIS HALFE PENNY. (½)

334. **O.** AT. THE. SHIP. TAVERNE = A ship. **R.** IN. GREENWIG. 1649 = S. A. S. (¼)

335. **O.** GEORGE. SAXBEE. IN = G. S. S. **R.** GREENWEECH. 1650 = G. S. S. (¼)

336. **O.** IOHN. SHALLCROS. IN = An unicorn. **R.** EAST. GREENE-WICH = I. E. S. (¼)

337. **O.** CHRISTOPHER. SKAYF = AT THE STIL. **R.** IN. GRINWICH = A Still. (½)

338. **O.** THOMAS. TVDER. IN = An unicorn. **R.** GREENWITCH = T. A. T. (¼)

339. **O.** RICHARD. TVSTEN. AT. YE = A dragon passant **R.** IN. GREENWICH. 1667 = HIS HALFE PENY. R. E. T. (½)

340. **O.** IOHN. WARRELL. AT. THE. SHIP = A ship in full Sail. **R.** TAVERNE. IN. GREENWICH. 69 = HIS HALF PENY. I. A. W. (½)

341. **O.** IOHN. WARRELL. THE = A ship. **R.** TAVERNE. IN. GREEN-WICH = I. A. W. (¼)

At the end of the 19th century, the Ship was still one of the principal hotels in Greenwich.

GROOMBRIDGE

342. **O.** RICH. CVNSTABLE. MERCER = The Mercers' Arms. **R.** IN. GROOME. BRIDG. 1665 = HIS HALF PENY. (½)

343. A variety is dated 1666. (½)

344. **O.** RICO. CONSTABLE. MERCR. 1668 = Mercers' Arms. **R.** = R. C. GROOM. BRIDG. ½D. (in four lines). (*Heart-shape*) (½)

HADLOW

345. **O.** = *John. Bateman. his. halfe. peny* (in four lines). **R.** IN. HAD-LOW. IN. KENT = A greyhound. (½)

At the end of the 19th century, an old inn at Hadlow still bore this sign; and the name of John Bateman appears in one of the church registers.

HARRIETSHAM

346. **O.** ROBRT. HOVENDEN. IN = The Grocers' Arms. **R.** HARY-ISOM. IN. KENT = R. I. S. the last two letters Conjoined. (¼)

HARTY

347. **O.** IOHN. GORGE. IN. HARTY = A man rowing a boat. **R.** IN. THE. ILE. OF. SHEPY = HIS HALF PENY. (½)

HAWKHURST

348. **O.** ARTHUR. GIBBONS = A gate. A. M. G. **R.** IN. HAWCKHERST. 1669 = HIS HALF PENY. (½)

349. **O.** IOHN. LATTER. BVCHER = HIS HALF PENY. **R.** OF. HAWKHVRST. IN. KENT = I. E. L. (½)

350. **O.** THOMAS. MERCER. CLOTHIER = HIS HALFE PENNY. **R.** OF. HAWKHERST. IN. KENT = T. A. M. (½)

351. **O.** WALTER. QVAIFE = A kind of arch. **R.** IN. HAWKHERST = HIS HALF PENY. W. E. Q. (½)

351.1 **O.** WALTER. QVAIFE = A kind of arch. **R.** IN. HAWKHERST = W. E. Q. (¼)

HIGH HALDEN

352. **O.** IOHN. COOKE. 1667 = HIS HALF PENY. **R.** IN. HIGH. HAL-DEN = A lion rampant. (½)

HOLLINGBOURNE

353. **O.** GEORGE. HARRISON = G. F. H. ½. **R.** IN. HOLLINGBVRNE = A windmill. (½)

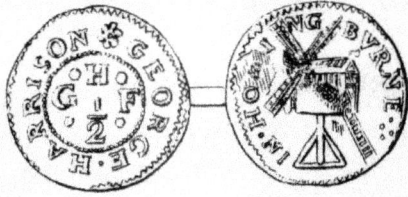

HONYCHILD (Parish of Hope, All Saints).

354. **O.** THE. MANNOR. OF = C. S conjoined (Charles Sedley). **R.** HONYCHILD. 1672= A goat's head, the Sedley family crest (½)

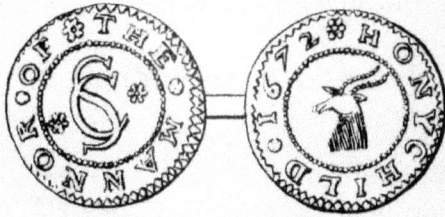

Sir Charles Sedley, Bart., who issued this token in the last vear they were allowed to circulate, shortly afterwards sold the manor of Honychild, distant one mile and a half from New Romney, in consequence of the injury he had done his estate by debauchery at the dissolute Court of Charles II. He was grandson of Sir William Sedley, the munificent founder of the Sedleian Lecture of Natural Philosophy at Oxford, and son of Sir John Sedley, of Aylesford. Sir Charles sat in the Long Parliament after the Restoration, and in three successive Parliaments, as well as during the reign of James II, whose attempts on the Constitution he vigorously withstood. He was active in bringing about the [Glorious] Revolution, which was the more extraordinary, as he had received favours from James II. The King, however, had taken a fancy to Catherine, the daughter of Sir Charles, whom he had made his mistress, creating her Countess of Dorchester. This honour greatly shocked Sir Charles, as, however debauched himself, he could not bear his daughter's dishonour. On being asked the cause of his conduct, he wittily remarked, "That as the King had made his daughter a countess, his gratitude compelled him to make the King's daughter a queen." Sir Charles lived many years after the Revolution, in the full possession of his wit and humour, dying at an advanced age. His works, which were of a licentious character, were published in two volumes, octavo.

HYTHE

355. **O.** WILLIAM. ADCOCK. IN = 1657. **R.** HEATH. IN. KENT. 57 = W. E. A. (¼)

356. **O.** FARDINANDO. BASSET = F. M. B. **R.** IN. HITHE. 1658 = A hart lodged. (¼)

The White Hart in High Street is still standing.

357. **O.** ION. BASSETT. HIS. HALF. PENY = I. T. B. 1670. **R.** IN. HYTH. IN. KENT = The Grocers' Arms. (½)

358. **O.** PETER. IOHNSON = The Bakers' Arms. **R.** OF. THE. PORT. OF. HID = P. I. (¼)

359. **O.** GVY. LANGDON. 1659 = The Grocers' Arms. **R.** IN. HETH = G. E. L. (¼)

360. **O.** DAVID. MARCH = A fleece. **R.** IN. HYTHE. 1669 = HIS HALF PENY. D. I. M. (½)

361. **O.** PETER. MARSH. 1672 = Arms. **R.** OF. HYTHE. IN. KENT = HIS HALF PENY. (½)

IGTHAM

362. **O.** = *Henry. Greene. His. Halfe. Penny* (in four lines). **R.** IN. IGHTHAM. IN. KENT = St. George and the dragon. (½)

363. **O.** IOHN. WAGGHORNE = The Mercers' Arms. **R.** IN. ITHAM. 1666 = I. M. W. (¼)

364. **O.** WILLIAM. WHITE = The Mercers' Arms. **R.** OF. ITHAM. IN. KENT = W. W. (¼)

LARKFIELD

367. **O.** IOHN. PACKE. AT. THE = The Blacksmiths' Arms. **R.** IN. LARCKFIELD. IN. KENT = HIS HALF PENY. (½)

LAMBERHURST

368. **O.** RICHARD. FRANCES = Arms; three chevrons. Crest, a greyhound. **R.** OF. LAMBVRHVRST. 1669 = R. A. F. HIS HALF PENY. (½)

LEEDS

369. **O.** NATHANIELL. BENSON = The Grocers' Arms. **R.** OF. LEEDS. IN. KENT = N. F. B. (¼)

369.1 **O.** IERIMY RVMFEILD = HIS HALF PENY. **R.** OF. LEEDS. 1670 = I. E. R. (½)

LENHAM

370. **O.** THO. AVSTEN. GROCER = The Grocers' Arms. **R.** OF. LEN-HAM. IN. KENT = T. A. A. (¼)

371. **O.** IOHN. DEEDE = A bear chained, with a dog baiting it. **R.** IN. LENHAM. 1664 = I. I. D. (¼)

An old inn at Lenham still displays the sign of the Dog and Bear.

372. **O.** THOMAS. FOORDE = The Grocers' Arms. **R.** IN. LENHAM. 1667 = HIS HALF PENY. (½)

373. **O.** IOHN LAKE = The Grocers' Arms. **R.** IN. LENHAM. 1667 = I. E. L. (¼)

LEWISHAM

374. **O.** IOHN. FREEMAN. AT. WHIT = A bear with chain, I. I. F. **R.** IN. LEWSAM. 1665 = HIS HALFE PENY. (½)

LYDD

375. **O.** THOMAS. EDERICKE = St. George and dragon. **R.** OF. LIDD. 1657 = T. E. (¼)

376. **O.** WILLIAM. SVDELL. OF = HIS HALF PENY. **R.** LIDD. IN. KENT. 1669 = W. F. S. (½)

377. **O.** WILLIAM. SVDELL = Three cloves. **R.** IN. LIDD. 1662 = W. S. (¼)

From the letters W. S we learn that the issuer was a bachelor in 1662, and from the letters W. F. S on the halfpenny of 1669 that he had married in that interval; also that his wife's Christian name commenced with F. The church registers do not record this event; but in the register of marriages, only two short years after the issue of his halfpenny, is: 1671. William Sudell, Esq., bayliff of Lydd, married Ann Knight, widdow. In the list of burials: 1676. January. Mrs. Sudell, the wife of William Sudell, juratt. There is no entry relating to the burial of William Sudell.

378. **O.** THO. WATERS. OF. LID. OR = T. W. **R.** APELDORE. IN. KENT = T. W. (¼)

379. A variety has the initials W. T. (¼)

MAIDSTONE

380. **O.** THOMAS. BOND. IN = The Grocers' Arms. **R.** MAYDSTONE. IN. KENT = T. L. B. conjoined. 1666. (¼)

381. **O.** ROB. BROOKE. IRONMONGER = HIS HALF PENY. **R.** IN. MAIDSTONE. 1670 = R. W. B. (½)

He was mayor in 1670, the same year he issued his halfpenny.

382. **O.** ROBERT. HEATH. OF = The Grocers' Arms. **R.** MAYDSTONE. GROCER = R. H. (¼)

PAS KENT-9B05E0

383. **O.** IOHN. HOAD. IN = A windmill. **R.** MEADSTONE. 1657 = I. H. (¼)

384. **O.** GERVIS. MAPLISDEN. OF = Arms; a cross pattée fitchée. **R.** MAIDESTONE. MERCER = HIS HALF PENY. (½)

PAS KENT-49DBE5

He was mayor more than once.

385. **O.** IAMES. RVSE. IN = The Grocers' Arms. **R.** MEYDSTONE. IN. KENT = I. R. (¼)

386. **O.** THOMAS. SWINOKE = Three men with astronomical instruments, standing round a globe. (This device is a symbol of the "World's End.") **R.** IN. MAIDSTONE = T. K. S. (¼)

A Thomas Swinnock was mayor in 1638.

387. **O.** IONATHAN. TROVGHTON = The Grocers' Arms. **R.** IN. MAIDSTON. 1668 = HIS HALF PENY. (½)

388. **O.** IONATHAN. TROVGHTON = The Grocers' Arms. **R.** IN. MAIDSTON. 1668 = I. M. T. (¼)

He was mayor during the Commonwealth.

389. **O.** RICHARD. WALKER = The Grocers' Arms. **R.** OF MAIDSTON. GROCER = R. W. 1658. (¼)

390. **O.** THOMAS. WALL. 1667 = The Salters' Arms. **R.** MAIDSTONE. HALFE. PENNY (in four lines across the field). (½)

390.1 **O.** THOMAS. WALL. 1667 = The Salters' Arms. **R.** MAID-STONE. HALFE. PENNY (*In lead*). (½)

391. **O.** RALPH. WARDE. IN = A castle. **R.** MAIDESTONE. 1656 = R. E. W. (¼)

392. **O.** IOHN. WATSON. AT. THE = A bell. **R.** IN. MAIDSTON. 1670 = HIS HALF PENY. (½)

393. **O.** ELIZABETH. WEBB = The Grocers' Arms. **R.** OF. MAID-STONE. GROCER = E. W. (¼)

394. **O.** WILLIAM. WEB. MERCER = The Grocers' Arms. **R.** IN. MAIDSTON. 1649 = W. E. B. (¼)

395. **O.** STEVEN. WEEKS. OF = The Weavers' Arms. **R.** MAIDSTONE. WEAVER = S. A. W. (¼)

396. **O.** WALTER. WEEKES. 1669 = HIS HALF PENY. **R.** IN. MAID-STONE. WEAVER = Weavers' Arms. (*Heart-shape*) (½)

397. **O.** RICHARD. WICKING = The Grocers' Arms. **R.** IN. MAID-STONE. GROCER = R. E. W. (¼)

398. **O.** IAMES. WOLBALL = The Grocers' Arms. **R.** OF. MAYDSTONE. 1664 = I. W. (¼)

399. A variety reads WOLBOLL. (¼)

MALLING

400. **O.** FRANCIS. CHAMBERS = The Grocers' Arms. **R.** IN. WEST. MALING = F. E. C. (¼)

401. **O.** RICH. CHAMBERS. OF = A fleur-de-lis. **R.** TOWNE. MAVLING. 1667 = R. M. C. (¼)

402. **O.** SAMVEL. FRENCH. OF. TOWN = 1668. **R.** MALLING. IN. KENT = S. I. F. (¼)

403. **O.** THOMAS. HILLS. 1668 = HIS HALF PENY. **R.** IN. TOVN. MAWLING. IN. KENT = T. I. H. (½)

MARGATE

404. **O.** GEORGE. FREIND. AT MARGRETT = Three pipes. **R.** IN. THE. ILE. OF. THANETT = G. M. F. (¼)

405. **O.** STEVEN. GREEDIER = HIS HALF PENY. **R.** OF. MARGET. IN. THANNET = The Fishmongers' Arms. (½)

406. **O.** CHRESTON. HOVDGBEN = A trade or merchant's mark. **R.** OF. MARGET. IN. KENT = C. H. (¼)

407. **O.** IOSEPH. IEWELL. 1669 = A cheese-knife. **R.** IN. MARGITT. IN. KENT = HIS HALF PENY. I. E. I. (½)

408. **O.** RICHARD. LANGLEY = The Tallowchandlers' Arms. **R.** AT. MARGET. IN. KENT = HIS HALFE PENY. 1667. (½)

409. A variety reads IN. TENIT. (½)

410. **O.** IOSEPH. MACKRITH. OF = A sugar-loaf. **R.** MARGERET. IN. KENT = I. I. M. (¼)

411. **O.** SARAH. READE. OF = A ship. **R.** MARGIT. IN. CENT = S. R. (¼)

412. **O.** WILLIAM. SAVAGE = The Grocers' Arms. **R.** OF. MARGET. IN. KENT = W. S. (¼)

413. **O.** IOHN. SKINNER. 1670 = A boat with sail. **R.** IN. MARGITT. IN. KENT = HIS HALF PENY. (½)

MILTON-NEXT-GRAVESEND

414. **O.** WILLIAM. BALDWIN = HIS HALF PENY. **R.** IN. MILLTON. 1667 = Two fleurs-de-lis. (*Heart-shape*) (½)

415. **O.** RICHARD. BUNCE = The Grocers' Arms. **R.** OF. MILTON. 1668 = HIS HALF PENY. (½)

416. **O.** GEORGE. HEAD. OF MILTON = A ship in full Sail. **R.** NEXT. GRAVES END. 1669 = HIS HALF PENY. G. M. H. (½)

417. **O.** IOHN. IONES. IN. MILTON = A cross pattée **R.** NEERE.
GRAVESEND = I. M. I. (¼)

418. **O.** WILLIAM. KEMSTER = Two bunches of grapes. **R.** OF. MILL-
TON. 1668 = HIS HALF PENY. (*Heart-shape*) (½)

William Kemster's name occurs in the assessment of Milton-next-
Gravesend on the parishioners, in 1687.

419. **O.** WALTER. NINN = The Bakers' Arms. **R.** IN. MILTON. 1666 =
W. N. (¼)

Ninn was Mayor of Gravesend in 1679, and again in 1694.

420. **O.** GEORGE. OLLEVER. IN = A sugar-loaf. **R.** MILTON. NEXT.
GRESEND = G. A. O. (¼)

He was mayor in 1680.

421. **O.** EDWARD. PASHLOWE = A rose. **R.** IN. MILLTON. 1656 = E. P. (¼)

He was Mayor of Gravesend and Milton in 1653.

422. **O.** WILLIAM. READE. IN. MILTON = The Pewterers' Arms. **R.** NEERE. GRAVESEND. 1666 = HIS HALF PENY. (½)

423. **O.** WILL. READ. IN. MILTON = The Pewterers' Arms. **R.** NEAR. GRAVES END = W. M. R. (¼)

424. **O.** IAMES. RICHMOND. OF = The Glaziers' Arms. **R.** MILTON. IN. KENT. 1666 = HIS HALF PENY. (½)

425. **O.** ANTHONY. SIFFLET. IN = A large ball. **R.** MILTON. NEXT. GRAVSEND = A. A. S. (¼)

426. **O.** IOHN. SMITH. OF. MILTON = A bird. **R.** NEERE. GRAVES-END = I. E. S. (¼)

427. **O.** ARTHVR. WHITE. AT. THE = An angel. **R.** MILTON. NERE. GRAVES END = A. M. W. (¼)

White was mayor in 1658.

MILTON-NEXT-SITTINGBOURNE

428. **O.** WILLIAM. ALLEN = The Bakers' Arms. **R.** IN. MILLTEN. 1658 = W. P. A. (¼)

429. **O.** WILLIAM. BISSY. IN = The Grocers' Arms. **R.** MILLTON. MERCER = W. I. B. (¼)

430. A variety reads WILLAM, etc. (¼)

431. **O.** CHENY. BOVRNE. OF = A sugarloaf. **R.** MILTON. IN. KENT = C. F. B. (¼)

432. **O.** WILLIAM. COVALL. IN = The Brewers' Arms. **R.** MELTON. IN. KENT. 1659 = W. M. C. (¼)

433. A variety is dated 1664. (¼)

434. **O.** RICHARD. HENMAN = A talbot. **R.** OF. MILTON. IN. KNT = R. S. H. (¼)

435. **O.** GEORGE. REEVE = The Grocers' Arms. **R.** OF. MILTON. 1667 = HIS HALF PENY. G. R. (½)

Several of these names are on the church registers.

MINSTER

436. **O.** IOHN. DYER = HIS HALF PENY. **R.** OF. MINSTER. IN. KENT = A sugar-loaf. (½)

NEWINGTON

437. **O.** THOMAS. BOORN. GROCER = The Grocers' Arms. **R.** AT. NEWINGTON. IN. KENT = HIS HALF PENY. 1669. (½)

437.1 **O.** LAWRENCE SHORT = The Fruiterers' Arms. **R.** IN NEWING-TON. = L. E. S. (¼)

438. **O.** WILLIAM. STANINOVGH. OF = The Mercers' Arms. **R.** NEW-INGTON. IN. KENT. MERCER = HIS HALF PENY. 1669. (½)

NORTHFLEET

439. **O.** THOMAS. HVMFRE. IN = A beehive. **R.** NORTH. FLEETE. IN. KENT = T. H. E. (in One line) (¼)

PAS LON-7121B2

440. **O.** ROBERT. PEACOCKE. AT = A crown. **R.** IN. NORTHFLEET. 1670 = HIS HALF PENY. (½)

ORPINGTON

441. **O.** IAMES. WHITE. IN. 1669 = The Blacksmiths' Arms. **R.** ORP-INGTON. IN. KENT = HIS HALF PENY. I. M. W. (½)

442. **O.** IAMES. WHITE. IN = The Blacksmiths' Arms. **R.** ORPINGTON. IN. KENT = I. M. W. (¼)

OTFORD

443. **O.** WILL. PHILLIPS. MERCER = The King's head crowned. **R.** IN. OTFORD. 1668 = HIS HALF PENY. (½)

PENSHURST

444. **O.** HENRY. CONSTABLE. OF = A crown. **R.** PENHVRST. IN. KENT. MERCER = HIS HALF PENY. 1667. (½)

445. A variety is dated 1669. (½)

446. **O.** MARTEN. PYKE. OF = A fleur-de-lis. **R.** PENSHVRST. MERCER = M. A. P. (¼)

PLUCKLEY

447. **O.** EDWARD. GOODING. OF = The Grocers' Arms. **R.** PLVCKLEY. IN. KENT. 1663 = E. A. G. (¼)

QUEENBOROUGH

448. **O.** HVMPHRY. ATWEEKE. AT. YE = A crown. **R.** IN. QVEENBOROVGH. 1667 = HIS HALF PENY. (½)

449. **O.** PETER. KEN. OF QVEEN = A rose. **R.** BOROUGH. IN. KENT = P. K. 1665. (¼)

450. **O.** THOMAS. NORRINGTON. IN = A ship in full sail **R.** QVINBOROVGH. IN. KENT = HIS HALFE PENNY. T. M. N. (½)

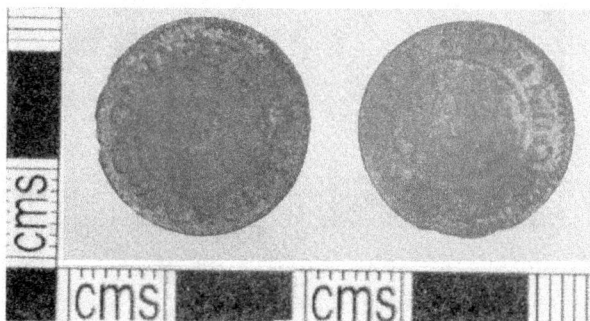

451. **O.** RICHARD. POLEY. OF = The Grocers' Arms. **R.** QVEINBOROVGH. 1666 = HIS HALFE PENNY. (½)

RAMSGATE

452. **O.** RICHARD. LANGLEY = A man making candles. **R.** OF. RAMSGATE. 1657 = R. P. L. (¼)

453. **O.** CLEMENT. MARCH. AT = A cheese-knife. 1658. **R.** ROMANSGAT. IN. THANET = C. M. M. (¼)

454. **O.** HEN. NOLDRED. IN. ROMANS = Three rolls of tobacco **R.** GET. IN. YE. ISLE. OF. TENNET = HIS HALF PENY. (½)

RIVERHEAD (Parish of Sevenoaks)

455. **O.** AT. THE. OKENTRE. 1653 = R. S. **R.** AT. RETHERED. IN. KENT = An Oak-tree. (¼)

PAS LON-27B0D7

ROCHESTER

456. **O.** GEORGE. ALLINGTON = The King's head. **R.** OF. ROCHES-TER = G. A. (¼)

The King's Head Inn is still standing in High Street, and has been known by this sign for over 450 years.

457. **O.** STEPHEN. BONNET. IN = The Joiners' Arms. **R.** ROCHESTER. EASTGATE = S. A. B. (¼)

458. **O.** ART. BROOKER. AT. THE = A crown. **R.** CROWNE. IN. ROCHESTER = A. M. B. (¼)

The Crown Inn is situated in High Street. There has been a house with this sign on the same spot for upwards of 600 years.

459. **O.** WILLIAM. BVRGES = 1669. **R.** OF. ROCHESTER = W. M. B. (¼)

460. **O.** WILLIAM. CAMPIAN = Two swords crossed **R.** IN. ROCHES-TER. 1658 = W. F. C. (¼)

461. **O.** ROBERT. CART = 1668. **R.** OF. ROCHESTER = R. S. C. (¼)

462. **O.** ROBERT. CHVRCHELL = The Merchant-Taylors' Arms. **R.** IN. ROCHESTER. 1669 = R. I. C. (¼)

463. **O.** ALICE. COBHAM = The Arms of the Cobham family; on a chevron three crescents. **R.** IN. ROCHESTER. 1651 = Crest of the Cobham family; a hind's head within a mural crown, A. C. (¼)

PAS LON-F97DB1

464. A variety is without A. C. on reverse. (¼)

465. **O.** S. IOHN. COBHAM. 1666 = The Cobham Arms. **R.** IN. ROCHESTER = Cobham crest, I. C. (¼)

466. **O.** EDWARD. HARRISON = A hand holding scissors. **R.** IN. ROCHESTER. 1669 = HIS HALF PENY. (½)

467. **O.** RICHARD. HVTCHESON = Three doves. **R.** IN. ROCHESTER = R. F. H. (¼)

468. **O.** IOHN. KENNON = A nag's head. **R.** OF. ROCHESTER = I. K. (¼)

The Nag's Head is still a well-known house in the town.

469. **O.** ROBERT. LEAKE = Arms. **R.** OF. ROCHESTER. 1656 = R. E. L. (¼)

470. **O.** ANTHONYE. LOVELL. AT. THE = Full-face of Henry VIII **R.** KINGS. HEAD. IN. ROCHES = A. L. (¼)

471. **O.** ANTHONY. LOVELL = Bust of Queen Elizabeth I. **R.** IN. ROCHESTER. 1657 = A. A. L. (¼)

472. **O.** ROBERT. MICHELL = Two compasses crossed **R.** OF. ROCHESTER = R. R. M. (¼)

473. A variety reads ROCHASTER.

474. **O.** RICHARD. NEWBERY = A black-jack. **R.** OF. ROCHESTER. 1666 = R. M. N. (¼)

475. **O.** THOMAS. PALMER = A Still. **R.** IN. ROCHESTER = T. E. P. (¼)

475.1 **O.** THOMAS. PIGOTT AT Y = A man greeting a woman (Salutation). **R.** IN. ROCHESTER = T. S. P. (¼)

476. **O.** EDWARD. SHELLEY = The Queen of Bohemia's head crowned. **R.** OF. ROCHESTER. CVRY = E. F. S. (¼)

477. **O.** SAMVELL. STOWE. THE = The Prince of Wales' feathers **R.** POST. OF. ROCHESTER = S. E. S. (¼)

478. **O.** IOSEPH. TRAVERS = Tobacco-roll and four pipes. **R.** IN. ROCHESTER. 1666 = I. G. T. (¼)

479. **O.** WILLIAM. VANDALL. IN = A lion couchant and sun. **R.** ROCHESTER. HIS. HALF. PENY = W. I. V. 1671. (½)

480. **O.** GILBERT. YOVNG. GROCR = A bell. **R.** IN. ROCHESTER. 1664 = S. Y. (¼)

PAS LON-D6CCDC

The names of Palmer and Young are still to be found in Rochester.

ROLVENDEN

481. **O.** IOHN. PEMBALL. 58 = I. M. P. **R.** ROLVENDEN. CHVRCH = A view of the church. (¼)

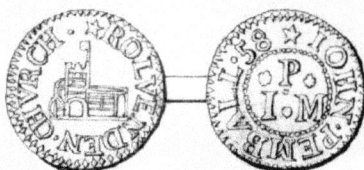

ROMNEY

482. **O.** RICHARD. BAKER = The Grocers' Arms. **R.** IN. NEW RVMNEY = R. M. B. (¼)

He was Mayor of New Romney in 1650 and 1655. The church registers of the town commence with the entry of his marriage: Nuptias solennes... etc. Ao 1662. Richardus Baker et Amisia Mundus, Vidva Jan. 28. The register of deaths records that in 1665 Richard Baker was bowried May 2. He must have been married twice. His son Richard, who was eight times mayor of the town, died in 1725, aged 74.

483. **O.** ISAAC. RVTTON. AT. YE. GEORG = St. George and dragon. **R.** IN. NEW. RVMNAY. IN. KENT = HIS HALF PENY. (½)

RYARSH

484. **O.** EDW. WALSINGHAM. 68 = HIS HALF PENY. **R.** IN. RYARSH. IN. KENT = A harrow. (½)

ST. MARY CRAY

485. **O.** ANN. MANING. IN. S = A boy holding a pipe. **R.** MAREY. CRAY. IN. KENT = A. M. 1658. (¼)

486. A variety is dated 1665. (¼)

At the end of the 19th century, the Black Boy was the leading hotel in St. Mary Cray.

487. **O.** EDWARD. SPURLING. OF = A mounted cannon. **R.** S. MARY. CRAY. IN. KENT = E. A. S. (¼)

SANDHURST

488. **O.** IOHN. OWEN. HIS. HALF. PENY. OF = Three crowns on the royal oak. **R.** SANDHVRST. IN. KENT = O. below 1669. (*Heart-shape*) (½)

SANDWICH

489. **O.** RICHARD. ASHERNIDEN = R. S. A. **R.** OF. SANDWICH = R. S. A. (¼)

490. **O.** ANNE. ATKINS. WIDOW = A carnation flower. **R.** OF. SAND-WICH. 1667 = A. A. (¼)

491. **O.** IOANNA. AVSTIN = I. A. **R.** IN. SANDWICH. 1656 = I. A. (¼)

591. **O.** W. B. **R.** = A bird in a shield. (*in lead*) (¼)

492. **O.** GEORGE. BVRFORD = The Grocers' Arms. **R.** OF. SAND-WICH. 1666 = HIS HALFE PENNY. (½)

493. **O.** IOHN. CASBE = HIS HALF PENY. **R.** IN. SANDWICH = A fleur-de-lis. (½)

A tavern in Sandwich still bears this sign.

494. **O.** RICHARD. CLARKE = The Prince of Wales' feathers. **R.** IN. SANDWICH. 1656 = R. A. C. (¼)

495. **O.** IOHN. COVCHMAN = I. E. C. **R.** IN. SANDWICH. 1656 = I. E. C. (¼)

496. **O.** RICHARD. CRISP = Two swords crossed. **R.** IN. SANDWICH = R. C. (¼)

497. **O.** IOSEPTH. DOE = HIS HALF PENY. **R.** OF. SANDWICH = A man making candles. (½)

498. **O.** HENRY. FVRNICE. IN = HIS HALF PENY. **R.** SANDWICH = The Arms of the Town of Sandwich; per pale three demi-lions passant gardant, conjoined in pale with as many demi-hulks of ships. (½)

499. **O.** HENRY. FVRNICE. IN = SANDWICH. **R.** (*No legend*) = The Arms of Sandwich as before. (¼)

Henry Furnese was a sergeant of dragoons, and married Ann, daughter of Mr. Andrew Gosfright, one of the jurats of Sandwich. Upon his marriage he settled in the town as a grocer and tallowchandler in a small house on the west side of the fish market, in which their son, afterwards Sir Henry Furnese, was born. This house was pulled down in 1786, and the ground formed part of the site of the Rose Inn. He was admitted a freeman of the corporation, December 10, 1657, and died June 12, 1672, aged 43.

500. **O.** THOMAS. KINGSFORD = HIS HALF PENY. **R.** OF. SAND-WHICH = POST MASTER. (½)

1569. A common post for carriage of letters appointed. 1661. The mayor and jurats solicit the Duke of York for a continuance of the privilege of a foot post, to carry money and goods to and from Sandwich, Deal, and London, according to ancient custom, notwithstanding the Act of Parliament for creating the post-office — **Annals of Sandwich**.

501. **O.** DANILL. PICHLEY = D. S. P. **R.** IN. SANDWICH. 1656 = D. S. P. (¼)

502. **O.** IOHN. REVELL = HIS HALF PENY. **R.** IN. SANDWICH = A bell. (½)

1669. The King, Duke of York, Prince Rupert, and the Earl of Sandwich came to town and the mayor presented the king with a glass of sack at the Bell Tavern door, which the king drank on horseback. — **Annals of Sand-wich**. The Bell, the principal inn at the end of the 19th century, still stands.

503. **O.** IAMES. ROBINS = Arms. **R.** IN. SANDWICH 1655 = I. R. (¼)

592. **O. R. R.** (Ralph Robins). **R.** = A sailing-boat. (*In lead*) (¼)

504. **O.** RALPH. ROBINS = A boat with rigging. **R.** IN. SANDWICH. 1655 = R. S. R. (¼)

505. A variety reads RALFH, etc. (¼)

506. **O.** DAVID. ROGERS = A bunch of grapes. **R.** IN. SANDWICH = D. I. R. (¼)

507. **O.** THOMAS. SANDVM = HIS HALF PENY. A spade and hoe crossed. **R.** IN. SANDWICH. 1667 = T. S. A tree. (½)

507.1 **O.** *David Tvrnvr* **R.** *Qvarter of an ovnce of fine pewter.* (*In lead*) (¼)

508. **O.** IOHN. VANDEBROVCK = A merchant's mark: "Lacy's Knot." **R.** IN. SANDWICH. 1656 = I. D. B. V. (¼)

593. **O.** = W. A merchant's mark over. **R.** = A pelican feeding its young. (*In lead*) (¼)

The Pelican Tavern has long ceased to hold a place in the street to which it has left a name. In a list of quit rents of lands, etc, belonging to St. Peter's Church, Sandwich, collected between the years 1646 and 1661, there is: 1646. The Widow White for house in the High Streete, 3s. 4d., formerly the Three Mariners, now the Pelican. The letter W. on the obverse favours the idea that this token was issued by the Widow White.

509. **O.** THOMAS. YOVNG. 1666 = A roll of tobacco. **R.** IN. SAND-WICH. IN. KENT = T. M. Y. (¼)

SEVENOAKS

510. **O.** WILLIAM. ALLEN. OF = The Grocers' Arms. **R.** SEAVENOCKS. IN. KENT = W. A. (¼)

511. **O.** NICHOLAS. BROOKSED = A pistol. N. M. B. **R.** IN. THE. SEVEN. OAKES = HIS HALF PENY. (½)

512. **O.** RICHARD. CRONKE. 1658 = The Merchant-Tailors' Arms. **R.** AT. SEAVEN. OAKES. KENT = R. M. C. (¼)

513. **O.** DANIELL. DAVES. 1668 = A bell. **R.** IN. SEVENOAKS. IN. KENT = HIS HALFE PENNY. (½)

514. **O.** DANIEL. DAVIS. 1666 = CHEESMONGER. **R.** IN. SEAVEN. OAKS. IN. KENT = D. D. D. (¼)

515. **O.** THOMAS. GREEN. OF. 1668 = The Mercers' Arms. **R.** SEAVENOKS. IN. KENT = HIS HALF PENY. T. C. (½)

516. **O.** THOMAS. GREENE. OF = The Mercers' Arms. **R.** SEVENOAKES. IN. KENT = T. G. (¼)

517. **O.** = NATHLL. OWEN. OF. SEAVEN. OAKES. MERCER (in five lines). **R.** = HIS. HALFE. PENNY. 1669. N. E. O. (in six lines). (*Octagonal*) (½)

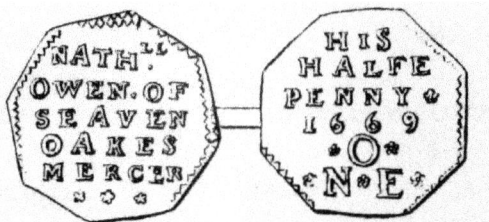

Nathaniel Owen was committed to Maidstone Gaol for refusing to bear arms as a soldier.

518. **O.** IOHN. THORNTON. 65 = A bull. **R.** IN. SEAVEN. OAKES = I. T. (¼)

519. **O.** WILL. WALL. AT. SEAVENOAKS = Three sugar-loaves. **R.** IN. KENT. HIS. HALFE. PENY = W. M. W. 1668. (½)

520. **O.** WILLIAM. WALL. IN = Three sugar-loaves. **R.** SENOCKE. IN. KENT = W. W. 1666. (¼)

521. **O.** THOMAS. WICKENDEN = 1666. **R.** SEVEN. OAKES. IN. KENT = T. I. W. (¼)

SHEERNESS

522. **O.** RICHARD. IONES. SVTLER = HIS HALF PENY. **R.** OF. SHIR-NESS. 1667 = R. I. (½)

SHURLAND

523. **O.** SHURLAND. IN. KENT. SHEPPIE = The crest of the Herbert family; a wyvern. **R.** (*No legend*) = The arms of Herbert; three lions rampant; impaling Spiller, a cross between four mullets. (½)

James Herbert, sixth son of Philip, fourth Earl of Pembroke and Montgomery, and Baron Herbert of Shurland, married Jane, daughter of Sir Robert Spiller of Laleham, county of Middlesex. Their arms are impaled on the token issued at Shurland, which is in the parish of Eastcheap, in the Isle of Sheppey; the manor of Shurland appears to have been settled on James Herbert on his marriage. He was knight of the shire for Oxford. His name appears as a subscriber to Harris' **History of Kent**, in 1709.

SITTINGBOURNE

524. **O.** IOHN. MILWAY. IN. SITTING = Three doves. **R.** BORNE. NEXT. THE. CROWN = I. M. M. (¼)

525. **O.** THOMAS. PEARCE. 1667 = The Ironmongers' Arms. **R.** IN. SITTINBORNE. KENT = HIS HALF PENY. T. P. conjoined. (½)

526. A variety is dated 1669. (½)

527. **O.** WILLIAM. WEBB. AT. THE = St George and dragon. **R.** IN. SITTINGBORN. 1670 = HIS HALF PENY. (½)

SMARDEN

528. **O.** THOMAS. HINCKLY. IN = A gate **R.** SMERDEN. IN. KENT. 1669 = HIS HALF PENY. T. S. H. (½)

PAS KENT-415632

SNAVE

529. **O.** THOM. BRETT. OF. SVEAFE = A fleur-de-lis. **R.** IN. RVMNEY. MARSH = A fleur-de-lis. T. B. (¼)

SOUTHFLEET

529.1 **O.** IOHN GARLAND = Catherine-wheel. (*In lead*) (¼)

SPELDHURST

530. **O.** THO. SOANE. MERCER. 1668 = An unicorn. **R.** IN. SPELDHVRST. IN. KENT = HIS HALF PENY. (½)

STOKE

531. **O.** WILLIAM. GILBART = A sugar-loaf. **R.** AT. STOAKE. IN. KENT = W. G. (¼)

STROOD

532. **O.** HENRY. ALLEN. AT. THE = A bulls head. **R.** CASTEL. IN. STROOD = A castle (¼)

533. **O.** EDWARD. BERBLOCKE = The Grocers' Arms. **R.** IN. STROVD. IN. KENT = E. M. B (¼)

534. **O.** = *Robert. Coverdale. at. Strovd* (in three lines). **R.** = *His. Halfe. Peny.* 1668. R. H. C. (in four lines). (½)

535. **O.** PHILLIP. EWER. OF = P. E. **R.** STROOD. IN. KENT = 1652. (¼)

535.1. A variety has the date 1651. (¼)

536. A variety has the date 1666. (¼)

537. **O.** HENNERE. FIGGETT = H. M. F. **R.** OF. STROOD. IN. KENT = 1654. (¼)

538. **O.** ANTH. LOVELL. IN. STROVD = An angel **R.** NEERE. ROCH-ESTER = A. S. L. 68. (¼)

539. **O.** CONSTANCE. WALSALL = A bird. **R.** IN. STROVD. IN. KENT = A still (¼)

540. **O.** CONSTANT. WALSALL = A Still. **R.** OF. STRVDE. IN. KENT = C. W. 1666. (¼)

541. **O.** CONSTANT. WALSALL = A Still. **R.** IN. STRVD. 1667 = W. C. (¼)

STURRY

542. **O.** THOMAS. IHONSON = The Grocers' Arms. **R.** AT. STOOWRY. 1650 = T. I. A fleur-de-lis. (¼)

543. A variety has the name corrected to IOHNSON. (¼)

544. **O.** WILLIAM. PICARD. OF = W. E. P. **R.** STVRREY. IN. KENT. 1666 = HIS HALF PENY. (½)

SUTTON-AT-HONE

545. **O.** IOHN. CHILD. OF. SVTTON = Three wheatsheaves. **R.** AT. HONE. IN. KENT. 1667 = HIS HALFE PENNY. (½)

SUTTON VALENCE

Sutton Valence is the parish name; the village is sometimes called Town Sutton.

548. **O.** AT. THE. KINGS. HEAD = Full-face of Henry VIII **R.** IN. TOVN. SOVTTON = R. G. (¼)

549. **O.** ISAAC. HVNTT. OF = A lion rampant. **R.** TOWNE. SVTTON. 1671 = HIS HALF PENY. (½)

TENTERDEN

550. **O.** = IOHN. CHVRCH. IN. TANTERDENE. 1668 (in six lines). **R.** HIS. HALF. PENY = The Butchers' Arms. (*Octagonal*) (½)

550.1 **O.** = IOHN. CHVRCH. IN. TANTERDENE. 1668 (in six lines). **R.** HIS. HALF. PENY = The Butchers' Arms. (½)

551. **O.** IAMES. MEAD. 1667 = An angel. **R.** IN. TENTARDEN = HIS HALF PENY. (½)

552. **O.** IOHN. READER. OF = The Grocers' Arms. **R.** TENTERDEN. IN. KENT = I. R. (¼)

553. A variety reads: **R.** TENTERDEN. IN. SVSSEX = I. R. (¼)

TUNBRIDGE

554. **O.** = WILLIAM. FREEMAN. HIS. HALF. PENNY (in four lines). **R.** IN. TVNBRIDGE. 1667 = A roll of tobacco. W. E. F. (½)

555. **O.** WILLIAM. OVEREY. OF = HIS HALF PENY. **R.** TVNNBRIDG. IN. KENT = W. O. 1669. (½)

556. **O.** = *Stephen. Putland. his.* ½. 1666 (in four lines). **R.** IN. TVNBRIDGE = S. A. P. (½)

557. **O.** I. E. STRETFEILD. MERCERS = The Skinners' Arms. **R.** IN. REATHERF. &. TVNBRIDGE = I. E. S. (¼)

558. **O.** ROBERT. WALICE = The Butchers' Arms. **R.** OF. TVNBRIDGE = R. W. (¼)

559. **O.** = RICHARD. WOOD. HIS. HALF. PENNY (in four lines). **R.** = IN. TVNBRIDG. IN. KENT. 1668 (in four lines). (½)

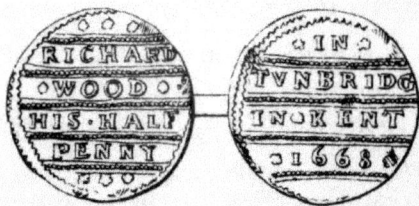

560. **O.** RICHARD. WOOD = R. W. **R.** OF. TVNBRIDGE = 1652. (¼)

561. **O.** RICHARD. WOOD. OF = A rose. **R.** TVNBRIDGE. IN. KENT = R. K. W. (¼)

WATERINGBURY

562. **O.** IOHN. CAREY. GROSER = 1669. **R.** OF. WOTERENBVRY. KENT = I. C. (¼)

WESTERHAM

563. **O.** SAMVELL. DALLING. OF = S. A. D. **R.** WESTERHAM. IN. KENT = 1653. (¼)

564. A variety reads DAILLING. (¼)

565. Another variety has the date 1664 (¼)

566. **O.** ANTHONY. SAXBEY. OF = A man making candles. **R.** WESTERHAM. IN. KENT = A. A. S. (¼)

WESTGATE (Canterbury)

567. **O.** IOHN. WRAIGHTE = HIS HALFE PENNY. **R.** IN. WESTEGATE. 1668 = I. R. W. conjoined. (½)

WILLESBOROUGH

568. **O.** FRANCIS. BARTHOLOMEW = **R.** WILLESBOROVGH = HIS HALF PENNY. (½)

WINGHAM

569. **O.** IOHN. SOLLEY. IN = A lion rampant **R.** WINGHAM. IN. KENT = I. P. S. (¼)

WOODCHURCH

570 **O.** THO. BRISENDEN. OF = The Butchers' Arms. **R.** WOODCHVRCH. IN. KENT = HIS HALF PENY. (½)

WOOLWICH

571. **O.** SARAH. BOWYER. OF. WOOLLWICH = A cannon mounted **R.** HER. HALFE. PENNY. 1667 = S. B. (½)

572. O. AT. THE. BARBERS. POLE = **R.** IN. WOOLEDGE. 1656 = W. I. F. (¼)

572.1 **O.** IOHN. HVTCHINS = A pair of scales **R.** IN. WOOLLEDGE. 1667 = I. E. H. (½)

573. **O.** IOHN. LADBROOKE = I. A. L. **R.** IN. WOOLLEDGE. 1666 = HIS HALFE PENNY. (½)

573.1 A variety reads LADDBROOCK. (¼)

573.2 **O.** WILLIAM MASON. **R.** IN. WOOLLEDGE. 1657 = W. R. M. (¼)

574. **O.** LODWICK. POOLE. IN = The Carpenters' Arms. **R.** WOOLL-WICH. 1650 = L. E. P. (¼)

575. **O.** AT. THE. STATES. ARMES = A harp. **R.** IN. WOOLEDGE. 1656 = E. S. (¼)

576. **O.** RICHARD. SCOTT. 1666 = The Carpenters' Arms. **R.** IN. WOOLWICH = R. M. S. (¼)

577. **O.** IANE. TAMPSELL. IN. WOOLLWICH = The Joiners' Arms. **R.** HER. HALFE. PENNY. 1667 = I. T. (½)

578. **O.** DENIS. WATERS = HER HALFE PENNY. **R.** IN. WOOL-WICH. 1667 = D. W. (½)

WROTHAM

579. **O.** CHARLES. ALLFREY = A boar's head. **R.** OF. WROTHAM = C. A. (¼)

580. **O.** THOMAS. CAVERLEY = The Merchant-Tailors' Arms. **R.** IN. ROOTHAM. 1666 = T. C. (¼)

Thomas Caverley's name occurs frequently in one of the church registers.

WYE

581. **O.** MARIE. ALLEN = M. A. **R.** IN. WYE. 1666 = HER HALF PENY. (½)

582. **O.** THOMAS. ALLEN. AT. THE = A Saracen's head **R.** SARASANS. HEAD. IN. WIE = T. R. A. (¼)

583. **O.** IOHN. COVLTER = The Grocers' Arms. **R.** GROCER. IN. WYE. 1652 = I. S. C. (¼)

584. **O.** THOMAS. DAN. WEAVER = A snake coiled. **R.** IN. WYE. 1652 = T. M. D. (¼)

585. **O.** RICHARD. WHITTINGHAM. IN. WYE. 1667 (In five lines). **R.** HIS. ½. PENY = A winged horse. (*Octagonal*) (½)

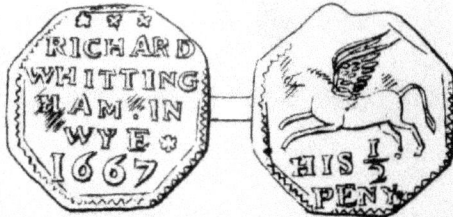

586. **O.** RICHARD. WHITTINGHAM = R. F. W. **R.** AT. THE. FLYING. HORSE = IN. WYE. (¼)

586.1 A variety reads: AT. THE. FLYING. HORSE VERY GOOD WINE

This is the oldest and formerly the principal inn of the interesting old town of Wye. The building remains but the inn has been replaced by the New Flying Horse on a different site.

YALDING

587. **O.** = DANIELL. CHILTENTEN. AT. YALDING. IN. KENT. 1668 (in five lines). **R.** = HIS. HALFE. PENY. D. A. C. (In five lines). (½)

588. A variety reads CHITTENDEN. (½)

589. **O.** GABRIEL. COVCHMAN = The Grocers Arms. **R.** OF. YALDING. IN. KENT = G. C. (¼)

6. EIGHTEENTH CENTURY TOKENS OF KENT

Anatomy of an Eighteenth — Nineteenth Century Token

Eighteenth and Nineteenth century tokens are considerably larger than seventeenth century tokens and usually struck on thick copper flans or discs, typically around two-three millimetres thick. A few trade tokens were struck in other metals such as brass and this is noted specifically in the listing. Diameter tends to match contemporary regal coinage, according to value although there are a few exceptions. Farthing tokens are typically 22mm in diameter; halfpenny tokens: about 27mm and penny tokens: around 34mm. Silver tokens again tend to match the diameter of regal values but not too consistently.

There were only 24 letters in the English alphabet until the eighteenth century, 'I' was used for both 'I' and 'J' while 'V' was used for both 'U' and 'V'. There has been a long-standing preference by coin and medal engravers to continue using the 24 letter alphabet, particularly the use of 'V' for 'U'. If you look at a British coin of George VI (1936-52), for instance, you will see the king's name rendered in Latin: GEORGIVS (pronounced Georgius). Tokens used both alphabets so if you are seeking to identify a token you look for the letters that appear on the tokens.

The thicker machine struck tokens included additional features over the earlier tokens in that many have an exergue, the name given to content, often a date, beneath a line horizontally dividing off the central design. The edge was now thick enough to be commonly engraved with lettering, like many of our top value coins today. As an alternative and sometimes an addition, edges were milled or engrailed. A Milled edge consists of regular marks, as on current higher value coins, except the milling was usually at an oblique angle rather than 90 degrees to the face. Engrailing is similar to milling but consists of a series of indents giving a serrated appearance. Most of the following images are from Charles Pye (1796) who as well as producing excellent engravings, ingeniously displayed the edge from the face of the token. Just to avoid any confusion, you cannot see the edge decoration from the face of the actual token.

In the listing of tokens which follows, the contractions used, are **O.** for the Obverse side of the Token, **R.** for the Reverse, **Ex.** for the Exergue and **E.** for the Edge. The = mark signifies that what follows is in the field or central part of the token; 1, ½, and ¼, signify Penny, Halfpenny and Farthing, showing the value of the token.

There is a convention of retaining the numbering from: R Dalton & S H Hamer. **The Provincial Token-Coinage of the 18th Century Illustrated** and W J Davis, **The Nineteenth Century Token Coinage of Great Britain, Ireland, The Channel Islands and The Isle of Man.** I have adhered to that convention here. As a result of new information there are a few additions which I have just indicated by placing a dash: '—' before the information.

The organisation of the token listings that follow are alphabetical order of place name using the 26 letter alphabet with modern spelling.

APPLEDORE

3. **O.** THE UNION OF APPLEDORE KENT. 1794. = A man carrying a sack to a windmill, and part of a house, in a beaded circle. **R.** PEACE INNOCENCE AND PLENTY = A lion and lamb lying together in standing corn. **E.** PAYABLE AT W. PECKHAM S APPLEDORE X. X. X. (½)

3a. As last but **E.** PAYABLE BY W. FRIGGLES GOUDHURST.

3b. As last but **E.** PAYABLE IN LANCASTER LONDON OR BRISTOL.

3c. As last but **E.** Plain.

Engraved by WYON. Manufactured by LUTWYCHE. Issuer: W. PECKHAM.

BENENDEN

4. **O.** PEACE AND PLENTY. = A wheatsheaf. **R.** BENENDEN HALF-PENNY. 1794 = Shield of arms. **E.** PAYABLE BY THOMAS REEVES BENENDEN + + + (½)

Only a small number of these tokens were circulated, the remainder being destroyed; there were originally four hundredweights. They are now rare.

4a. As last but **E.** PAYABLE BY F. HEATH BATH.

4b. As last but **E.** Plain.

Engraved by WYON. Manufactured by LUTWYCHE. Issuer: T. REEVES.

BROOKLAND

5. **O.** KENT HALFPENNY PAYABLE AT. = The Kentish horse in a beaded oval. **R.** GROCER AND DRAPER. 1794. = A cipher T K, over it a fleece. **E.** PAYABLE BY THOMAS KING'S BROOKLAND +. +. +. +. (½)

Engraved by ARNOLD. Manufactured by LUTWYCHE. Issuer: T. KING. This token is scarce.

CANTERBURY

6. **O.** UNITY PEACE AND CONCORD. GOOD WILL TO ALL MEN =
Side view of Canterbury Cathedral. **Ex.** CANTERBURY TOKEN in two
lines. **R.** PROTECTION TO OUR KING AND COUNTRY LAWS AND
TRADE + 1794 + = Shield of arms of the city of Canterbury and a mural
crown. **E.** PAYABLE AT JOHN MATTHEWS'S + + + + (½)

6a. As last but **E.** PAYABLE IN LANCASTER LONDON OR BRISTOL.

This is an artist's proof and probably unique.

7. **O.** and **R.** Same as No. 6. **E.** PAYABLE AT JAMES ROBERTSONS +
+ + (½)

Engraved by DIXON. Manufactured by LUTWYCHE. Issuer: J. MAT-
THEW.

8. **O.** CANTERBURY TOKEN. = Side view of Canterbury Cathedral. **Ex.**
a cipher E.P. **R.** OUR KING AND COUNTRY LAWS AND TRADE. +
1795 +. A Maltese cross before and after date. = Same arms and crown as
before. **E.** PAYABLE AT CANTERBURY + + + + (½)

8a. As last but **E.** Plain.

9. **O.** Similar to last, the cypher is larger, and there is no period at end of legend. **R.** and **E.** Same as last. (½)

9a. As last but **E.** Plain.

10. **O.** and **E.** Same as No. 9. **R.** Similar, but with a dot on each side of date in place of Maltese cross, and a dot in the legend after "COUNTRY." (½)

Engraved by DIXON. Manufactured by WARING. All these tokens, except no.7 are rare.

The initials E. P. refer to Edward Pillou, a Canterbury Tailor.

DEAL

11. **O.** THE GUARD & GLORY OF G' BRITAIN. = A man of war sailing. **R.** DEAL HALFPENNY TOKEN. = Shield of arms of the Cinque Ports, 1794 above shield. **E.** PAYABLE AT RICHARD LONG'S LIBRARY. X . (½)

11a. As last but **E.** MASONIC TOKEN I SCETCHLEY FECIT.

11b. As last but **E.** Plain.

11c. As last but **E.** AT RICHARD SHIPDENS.

— As last but **E.** PAYABLE IN LANCASTER LONDON OR BRISTOL.
Engraved by WYON. Manufactured by LUTWYCHE. Issuer: R. LONG.

DEPTFORD

12. **O.** KENTISH LIBERTY PRESERVED BY VIRTUE & COURAGE =
The Kentish men meeting William the Conqueror. **Ex.** 1067 **R.** PROS-
PERITY TO THE WOODEN WALLS OF OLD ENGLAND = The stern
of the "ROYAL GEORGE" **Ex.** KENT HALFPENNY 1795 T. H. D. **E.**
PAYABLE AT DEPTFORD CHATHAM AND DOVER. (½)

13. **O.** As last, but with flaw after die had cracked. **R.** Similar, but centre
lamp touches 'E' in WOODEN and water-line extends beyond ship nearly
to 'T' and 'D' in the legend. **E.** PAYABLE AT THO'S HAYCRAFTS
DEPTFORD. (½)

13a. As last but **E.** PAYABLE AT DEPTFORD CHATHAM AND DO-
VER.

14 **O.** Similar to No. 12 from new die with a small cross instead of a dot at end of legend; the 6 in date touches the exergue line. **R.** The centre lamp touches E; the waterline extends almost from I to D in the legend. **E.** PAYABLE AT DEPTFORD CHATHAM AND DOVER. (½)

Manufactured by MYND. Issuer: THOS. HAYCRAFT, Ironmonger.

DYMCHURCH

15. **O.** ROMNEY MARSH HALFPENNY. 1794 = A cipher W.P. crest a lamb. **R.** FOR THE HONOR AND USE OF TRADE. = Figure of Justice standing. **E.** PAYABLE AT W. PARRIS DIMCHURCH. X. X. X. (½)

15a. As last but **E.** Plain.

— As last but **E.** PAYABLE IN LANCASTER LONDON OR BRISTOL.

Some have "blundered" edge, thus—PARRDIMCHURCH.

Artist—WYON. Manufactured by LUTWYCHE.

DOVER

16. **O.** THE. R. HON. W. PITT LORD WARDEN CINQUE PORTS = Bust facing right. **R.** CINQUE PORTS TOKEN PAYABLE AT DOVER. = The arms of Dover. 1794. **E.** AT HORN'S LIBRARY. The remainder engrailed. (½)

16a. As last but **E.** PAYABLE IN LANCASTER LONDON OR BRISTOL.

16b. As last but **E.** PAYABLE AT LONDON OR DUBLIN.

16c. As last but **E.** PAYABLE BY I GIBBS LAMBERHURST.

16d. As last but **E.** PAYABLE AT W PARKERS OLD BIRMINGHAM WAREHOUSE.

16e. As last but **E.** PAYABLE AT RICHARD MAPLESDEN WINCHELSEA.

John Horn was a bookseller, stationer, perfumer, proprietor of the Apollo Circulating Library and Public Reading Room, and organist. Engraved by DIXON. Manufactured by LUTWYCHE.

17 **O.** R. HON. W. PITT LORD WARDEN CINQUE PORTS = Bust full face. **R.** Same as last. **E.** PAYABLE IN LANCASTER LONDON OR BRISTOL. (½)

18. **O.** Same as last. **R.** THE WOODEN WALLS OF OLD ENGLAND. = A ship sailing. **E.** PAYABLE IN LANCASTER LONDON OR BRISTOL (½)

18a. As last but **E.** PAYABLE IN LONDON. The remainder engrailed.

"A few impressions; the dies not being hardened, were immediately spoiled."

19. **O.** Dover Castle and a distant view of ships at sea. **Ex.** DOVER TOKEN. **R.** DEDICATED. TO. COLLECTORS. OF. PROVINCIAL. COINS. 1795. = Military trophy within a laurel wreath. **E.** PAYABLE IN LONDON. The remainder engrailed. (½)

— As last but **E.** Plain.

Engraved by Jacobs. Probably issued by Skidmore for sale to collectors.

FAVERSHAM

20. **O.** PAYABLE AT FEVERSHAM. = An ancient sloop. **R.** CINQUE PORT HALFPENNY. 1794. = Shield of arms of the Cinque Ports. **E.** PAYABLE AT IOHN CROWSS COPPER SMITH X . X (½)

20a. As last but **E.** PAYABLE IN LANCASTER LONDON OR BRISTOL.

20b. As last but **E.** Plain.

John Crow was a brazier [edge reading in error]. Engraved by DIXON. Manufactured by LUTWYCHE.

FOLKESTONE

21. **O.** PAYABLE. AT. FOLKSTONE. KENT. VALUE ONE. HALFPENNY. 1796. In two circles, with date in centre. **R.** MAY. COMMERCE. FLOURISH. = Ships lying at a quay. **E.** Milled over SKIDMORE, HOLBORN, LONDON. (½)

Probably made by Skidmore, for sale to collectors.

GODINGTON

22. O. GODINTON. HOP-TOKEN. 1767. = The name of Issuer, TOKE, in monogram. The top corners of the monogram point to the two T's of the legend. **R.** NO PAINS NO GAINS. = A basket heaped full of hops, no band round the basket. (*Also in brass*) (½)

23. O. GODINTON HOP TOKEN 1767. = TOKE, in monogram. The top corners of the monogram point to the first N of GODINTON and the P of HOP. **R.** NO PAINS NO GAINS (no dot after legend) = A basket level full of hops, with band round the basket. The handles of basket point above O and to I (*Also in silver and brass*) (½)

24. O. Similar to last. The top corners of the monogram point to T of "GODINTON" and P of "HOP" **R.** Similar to last. The handles of basket point to O and N. (*In brass*) (½)

25. **O.** Crest of the Toke family within a broad rim. **R.** Blank. (½)

26. **O.** Initials of John Toke within a broad rim. **R.** Blank. (½)

27. **O.** Similar to last, within a narrow rim. **R.** Blank. (½)

Possibly of late 19th century manufacture from an old pattern.

GOUDHURST

28. **O.** KENT HALFPENNY TOKEN = The Kentish horse. **Ex.** 1794. **R.** FOR GENERAL CONVENIENCE. = Shield of arms of the City of Canterbury. **E.** PAYABLE BY W. FRIGGLES GOUDHURST + + + + (½)

The name on the edge of this piece being spelt wrong, it was suppressed and when any are found, an attempt has usually been made to erase the name.

28a. As last but **E.** PAYABLE BY W. FUGGLES GOUDHURST. X. X. X. X

28b. As last but **E.** PAYABLE BY W. FUGGLES GOUDHURST + + + +

28c. As last but **E.** PAYABLE AT W. PECKHAM'S, APPLEDORE. + + +

29. **O.** and **R.** Same as last. **E.** PAYABLE BY W. MYNS GOUDHURST + + + + (½)

These pieces are found countermarked; 28a with an F and No. 29 with an M. William Fuggle was a tallow-chandler. William Mynn, a shopkeeper. Engraved by ARNOLD. Manufactured by LUTWYCHE.

GRAVESEND

1. **O.** GRAVESEND TOKEN. = A Gravesend boat sailing. **R.** NAVAL + PENNY. 17 + 97 = A crown and naval coronet between sprigs of laurel. **E.** Engrailed. (1)

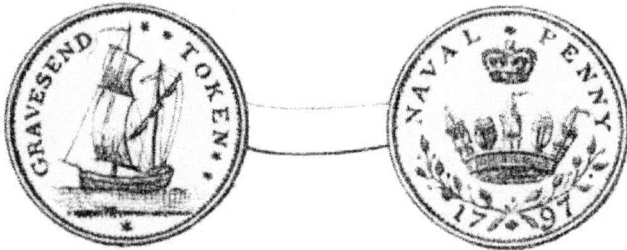

— As last but **E.** Plain.

— **O.** As last but **R.** Blank.

— **R.** As no. 1 but **O.** Blank.

This token is of small halfpenny size and is very rare. Issuer SKIDMORE.

HAWKHURST

30. **O.** HAWKHURST HALFPENNY PAYABLE AT = A cipher, C. H., crest a wheatsheaf. **R.** JUSTICE & CONFIDENCE THE BASIS OF TRADE. = The Kentish horse in a shield. **E.** CHARLES HIDER'S. The remainder milled. (½)

30a. As last but **E.** PAYABLE AT W. PARKERS OLD BIRMINGHAM WAREHOUSE.

HYTHE.

31. **O.** CINQUE PORT HALFPENNY. 1794. = Shield of arms of Cinque ports. **R.** PAYABLE AT HYTH. = An ancient sloop. **E.** AT RICHARD SHIPDEN'S . X . X . X . X . X (½)

31a. As last but **E.** MASONIC TOKEN I. SCETCHLEY FECIT. 1794. +

31b. As last but **E.** Plain.

Engraved by ARNOLD. Manufactured by LUTWYCHE.

LAMBERHURST

32. **O.** MAY HOPS FOR EVER FLOURISH. = A man picking hops, within a circle of dots. **R.** SUSSEX HALFPENNY TOKEN. 1794. = Shield of arms, between sprigs of leaves. **E.** PAYABLE BY T. FOSTER LAMBERHURST + + + + (½)

32a. As last but **E.** PAYABLE AT RICHARD MAPLESDEN'S WINCHELSEA. X . X .

33. **O.** Similar to last but the corner of the hop bin comes to the letter 'R' in FLOURISH instead of the letter 'U'. **R.** and **E.** The same as last. (½)

Both these tokens are very rare, as the obverse die of each appears to have failed after very few impressions.

34. **O.** Similar to last but the hop plants differ slightly, the legend more closely spaced and the corner of the hop bin comes near the letter 'S' in FLOURISH. **R.** and **E.** The same as last. (½)

35. **O.** FOR CHANGE NOT FRAUD. = Shield of arms of Chichester, SUSSEX on banner below. **R.** KENT HALFPENNY TOKEN. 1794. = Shield of arms of Canterbury. **E.** PAYABLE BY I. GIBB'S LAMBER-HURST + + + (½)

35a. As last but **E.** PAYABLE BY + I + GIBBS SUSSEX.

35b. As last but **E.** PAYABLE IN LANCASTER LONDON OR BRIS-
TOL.

35c. As last but **E.** PAYABLE BY M. LAMB & SON - - : - -

— As last but **E.** WARLEY CAMP HALFPENNY . X .

— As last but **E.** PAYABLE BY I GIBBS AMBERHURST

Designed by WYON. Manufactured by LUTWYCHE. Lamberhurst being
only a small town, partly in Kent and partly in Sussex, I Gibbs probably
had his place of business in the latter county, and, not to unduly favour
either, used the Arms of the county town of each.

MAIDSTONE

36. **O.** MAIDSTONE HALFPENNY. = 1795 above shield of arms and
supporters of the borough of Maidstone. **R.** THE SPRING OF FREEDOM
ENGLANDS. BLESSING = A figure of Justice standing. **Ex.** KENT. **E.**
PAYABLE BY HENRY OLIVERS + +

36a. As last but **E.** Plain.

— As last but **E.** Cancelled with overstamping.

37. **O.** MAIDSTONE HALFPENNY. = Shield of arms and supporters of the borough of Maidstone. **R.** PAYABLE BY J. SMYTH AT PADSOLE PAPERMILL 1795. = View of a paper mill. **E.** Milled. (½)

Henry Oliver was a cutler. James Smith is recorded in the Universal British Directory as being Agent to the Sun Fire Office. The writer of the "Bazaar Notes" states that SMYTH is the correct form. Engraved by DIXON. Manufactured by LUTWYCHE.

ORPINGTON

2. **O.** THEIR VALUE UPWARDS OF £500 = A hand firing a gun from left at startled horse, dead horses either side, shield of arms above, within circle **Ex.** TUTAMEN VOLUNTARILY DESTROY'D BY D. COLGATE OF ORPINGTON KENT 1795 (In six lines) **R.** A. MARK OF RESPECT TO THE RT. HON.T. SKINNER SR. R. GLODE KT. & MR. W. AUSTIN. = Arms of Kent, WE. ALSO ARE BUT AS YESTERDAY OUR DAYS A SHADOW HE TAKETH AWAY WHO CAN HINDER MAN (ALSO) GIVETH UP THE GHOST AND WHERE IS HE! JOB. (In nine lines) **E.** Plain. (*Also in silver.*) (1)

This is really a medal issued to encourage prevention of disease in horses.

ROMNEY

38. **O.** ROMNEY HALFPENNY TOKEN 1794. = Shield of arms of the town of Romney. **R.** THE SUCCESS = A small antique sloop, between sprigs of laurel. **E.** PAYABLE AT IOHN SAWYER'S ROMNEY. X. (½)

38a. As last but **E.** Plain.

John Sawyer, was a house carpenter and joiner. Designed by WYON. Manufactured by LUTWYCHE

SANDWICH

39. **O.** SANDWICH HALFPENNY TOKEN FOR = An ancient sloop. **R.** MANUFACTURERS TRADE AND COMMERCE. = Shield of arms of the Cinque Ports. **E.** PAYABLE AT THOMAS BUNDOCKS X . X . X . X (½)

39a. As last but **E.** PAYABLE AT LANCASTER LONDON OR BRISTOL.

39b. As last but **E.** BRIGHTON CAMP HALFPENNY.

39c. As last but **E.** Plain.

Thomas Bundock, junior, was a weaver and Member of the Common Council. Engraved by DIXON. Manufactured by LUTWYCHE.

STAPLEHURST

40. **O.** STAPLEHURST HALFPENNY 1794. = A cipher I.S. crest a stag's head. **R.** FOR CHANGE NOT FRAUD = The Kentish horse. **Ex.** 1794. **E.** PAYABLE BY I SIMMONS STAPLEHURST + + + + + + + (½)

According to the "Bazaar Notes," John Simmons was a freeholder of Staplehurst, and a tallow chandler by trade. Engraved by ARNOLD. Manufactured by LUTWYCHE. Two hundredweights made.

STONE

41. **O.** M. SNOW. HOP. FACTOR. STONE. 1797. = A cipher M. S. within a circle. **R.** HALFPENNY = A thistle between sprigs. **E.** COVENTRY TOKEN and a wavy line. (½)

41a. As last, but **E.** Plain.

Very rare. As Snow's name is not in the Kent Directory for the period, it is probably a specimen made for sale to collectors. Some tokens show traces of filing on the edge, which may account for some with plain edge.

42. **O.** TENTERDEN HALFPENNY 1796 = Shield of arms of the Brewers' Company **R.** A horse and dray, and part of a brew house. **Ex.** TO CHEER OUR HEARTS. **E.** PAYABLE AT I & T CLOAKES BREW HOUSE .X X. (½)

42a. As last, but **E.** BIRMINGHAM REDRUTH & SWANSEA.

42b. As last, but **E.** Plain

Engraved by DAVIS. Manufactured by GOOD.

7. NINETEENTH CENTURY TOKENS OF KENT

FOLKESTONE

O. IOHN BOXER FOLKESTONE 1811 = The arms of the Cinque Ports, three lions passant gardant, as many hulls of ships; crest, a royal crown; inscribed on a banner below: CINQ PORT TOKEN **R.** ONE SHILLING VALUE within an olive wreath. (*In silver*) (12 pence)

Engraved by Thomas Halliday.

8. BIBLIOGRAPHY AND RESOURCES

James Atkins, **The Tradesmen's Tokens of the Eighteenth Century**, (London, 1892)

William Boyne, **Tokens Issued in the Seventeenth Century in England, Wales, and Ireland by Corporations, Merchants, Tradesmen, etc.**, (London, John Russell Smith, 1858)

James Conder, **An Arrangement of Provincial Coins, Tokens, and Medalets, Issued in Great Britain, Ireland, and the Colonies**, (Ipswich, 1798)

Robert Peirce Cruden, **The History of The Town of Gravesend in the County of Kent And of The Port of London** (London, 1843)

R. Dalton, **The Silver Token-Coinage Mainly Issued Between 1811 and 1812** (Leamington Spa, 1922)

R Dalton & S H Hamer. **The Provincial Token-Coinage of the 18th Century Illustrated**, (3 vols., London, 1910-1918; Reprinted 1 vol., London, Seaby, 1967; Massachusetts, Quarterman, 1977; Cold Spring USA, Davisson's, 1990, 1996, 2004)

W J Davis, **The Nineteenth Century Token Coinage of Great Britain, Ireland, The Channel Islands and The Isle of Man; to Which are Added Tokens of Over One penny Value of Any Period**, (London, 1904; Reprinted, London, Seaby, 1969)

Michael Dickinson, **Seventeenth Century Tokens Of The British Isles And Their Values**, (London, Spink, 1986, 2004)

Portable Antiquities Scheme (PAS) http://www.finds.org.uk

Charles Pye, **Provincial Copper Coins or Tokens**, (London, 1796)

George C Williamson, **Tokens Issued in the Seventeenth Century in England, Wales, and Ireland by Corporations, Merchants, Tradesmen, Etc. A New and Revised Edition of William Boyne's Work**, (2 vols., London, Elliot Stock, 1889-91; Reprinted 3 vols., London, Seaby 1967; Reprinted 2 vols., New York, Burt Franklin, 1970)

8.1. GREAT BOOKS IN PRINT FROM THE SAME AUTHOR

THE SUCCESSFUL TREASURE HUNTER'S SECRET MANUAL: Discovering Treasure Auras in the Digital Age, Soft Cover, 210mm x 146mm, 68 pages, (True Treasure Books, 2009) ISBN 978 0 9550325 54

(Also an E-Book under the title: THE SUCCESSFUL TREASURE HUNTER'S SECRET MANUAL: How to Use Modern Cameras to Locate Buried Metals, Gold, Silver, Coins, Caches…)

CLEANING COINS & ARTEFACTS: Conservation * Restoration * Presentation, Soft Cover, 210mm x 146mm, 110 pages, (Greenlight Publishing, 2008) ISBN 978 1 897738 337

(Also an E-Book under the title: THE SUCCESSFUL TREASURE HUNTER'S ESSENTIAL COIN AND RELIC MANAGER: How to Clean, Conserve, Display, Photograph, Repair, Restore, Replicate and Store Metal Detecting Finds)

PERMISSION IMPOSSIBLE: Metal Detecting Search Permission Made Easy, Soft Cover, 210mm x 146mm, 52 pages, (True Treasure Books, 2007) ISBN 978 0 9550325 30 (Also an E-Book)

SITE RESEARCH FOR DETECTORISTS, FIELDWALKERS & ARCHAEOLOGISTS, Soft Cover, 250mm x 190mm, 160 pages, (Greenlight Publishing, 2006) ISBN 1 897738 285

SUCCESSFUL DETECTING SITES: Locate 1000s of Superb Sites and Make More Finds, Soft Cover, 250mm x 190mm, 238 pages, (Greenlight Publishing, 2007) ISBN 978 1 897738 306

THE SUCCESSFUL TREASURE HUNTER'S ESSENTIAL SITE RESEARCH MANUAL: How to Find Productive Metal Detecting Sites, (E-Book)

THE ESSENTIAL GUIDE TO OLD, ANTIQUE AND ANCIENT METAL SPOONS, Soft Cover, 210mm x 146mm, 88 pages, (True Treasure Books, 2008) ISBN 978 0 9550325 47 (Also an E-Book)

THE SUCCESSFUL TREASURE HUNTER'S ESSENTIAL DOWSING MANUAL: How to Easily Develop Your Latent Skills to Find Treasure in Abundance, Soft Cover, 210mm x 146mm, 60 pages, (True Treasure Books, 2005) ISBN 0 9550325 04

(Also an E-Book under the title: THE SUCCESSFUL TREASURE HUNTER'S ESSENTIAL DOWSING MANUAL: How to Easily Develop Your Latent Skills to Locate Gold, Silver, Coins, Caches…)

MY ANCESTOR LEFT AN HEIRLOOM: Discovering Heirlooms and Ancestors Through the Metalwork They Left Behind, Soft Cover, 210mm x 146mm, 84 pages, (True Treasure Books, 2011) ISBN 978 0 9550325 61

(Also an E-Book under the title: MY ANCESTOR LEFT AN HEIR-LOOM: Hunting Family History and Genealogy Treasure Through Metal Detecting Finds)

METAL DETECTING MADE EASY: A Guide for Beginners and Reference for All, Soft Cover, 210mm x 146mm, 128 pages, (True Treasure Books, 2014) ISBN 978 0 9550325 78 (Also an E-Book)

FAITHFUL ATTRACTION: How to Drive Your Metal Detector to Find Treasure (E-Book)

All books are available from True Treasure Books online at http://www.truetreasurebooks.net Also many are available at Amazon.co.uk, Kindle, Ebay.co.uk, Alibris, Smashwords.com most UK bookshops and Metal Detector Retailers

CONCLUSION

Thank you for buying this book. I am sure you will find this book useful for identifying your Kent tokens and finding out something about the people and places which issued them.

If you have any additions, corrections or comments I would pleased to hear from you. You can contact me at David@truetreasurebooks.net

Depending on perceived demand, I plan to produce further books on tokens covering other counties. I would be grateful for any feedback so you can help others learn how they can benefit from this book and help me learn how I can better serve my readers.

Thank you.

ABOUT THE AUTHOR

David Villanueva (1951-) was born in Birmingham, England, where he grew up. In the early 1970s his mother bought him a copy of Ted Fletcher's book, **A Fortune Under Your Feet**, which, together with David's great interest in history inspired him to buy a metal detector and take up treasure hunting as a hobby. Family stories about the origins and history behind David's Spanish surname also spawned the hobby of genealogy. A career move brought David to Whitstable in Kent, England, and it was here that David's love of history research developed into great success both in metal detecting and family history. In metal detecting, all sorts of coins and artefacts are found which then generates further research and interest. Tokens are one of David's favourite finds! A little later David felt the urge to put pen to paper and started writing articles for the two British metal detecting magazines – Treasure Hunting and The Searcher – which have published more than two dozens of David's articles between them. Success in writing articles soon led to David's first book: **The Successful Treasure Hunter's Essential Dowsing Manual: How to Easily Develop Your Latent Skills to Find Treasure in Abundance**, published in both digital format and paperback. To date, David has written a further fourteen books related to metal detecting, treasure hunting and family history.

###